Be The One!

Will

"Resilient Rose is a touching personal account
of overcoming loss and unthinkable tragedy.
Hope will always help you find a way through
the darkness. Kellibrew's fighting spirit is an
inspiration to me."
— **Shawn Harrison**
Actor from Family Matters

"William Kellibrew's book is more than wrenching.
His words are painfully honest. They are from a
young man that I watched grow up in the glare
of the Washington, DC media. That little boy
who always wore a suit found a faith, mixed with
education and determination, to become such a
testimony. He was in his 30's when he met Oprah
as a relentless advocate who was not afraid to tell
his story. But he endured so much to become a
courageous advocate for himself and other children
who are often collateral damage and innocent
victims of domestic violence."
— **Hamil Harris**
Former Washington Post reporter and
lecturer at Howard University

RESILIENT ROSE

The REBIRTH *of* DIGNITY

Memoir

BY:

WILLIAM KELLIBREW

Elliness
PUBLISHING

ellinesspublishing.com

Printed in the United States of America
Copyright © 2023 by William Clarence Kellibrew

Paperback ISBN 978-0-9825735-6-3
Ebook ISBN 978-0-9825735-7-0

Elliness
PUBLISHING

173 Saint Patrick's Drive, Suite 104,
Waldorf MD 20603
ellinesspublishing.com

Book cover design and interior layout by Juan Roberts

TABLE *of* CONTENTS

ACKNOWLEDGMENTS

This book journey took over 34 years to complete and is far from a comprehensive account of my life's journey. I will save those vignettes for another book.

Thank you to my entire family, closest and dearest friends, colleagues, mentors, teachers, professors, classmates, supporters, and anyone who made a difference in my life. It is because of you that I exist the way that I do—having had your support and love to help me along the way.

Thank you, Mama, for taking us in and making a way and to Grandma Rose Jones. Thank you to my sister and brothers, Rodney, Tony, Manyka "Nicci," and Da'Vone, for being on this journey of healing together. Thank you to my partner, JuRon, for your wisdom beyond your years and your unwavering guidance and support. Thank you to my uncles Kevin, Allen, George, Vance, Donnie, Reggie, Deon, my aunts Gilvina, Diane, Nita, and Tammy, my nieces Len'Nyka, Josiah, Manika, Jewel, my nephews James, Damari, and Delontae, cousins, and vast extended family. Thank you to our god-kids, Daria, Jasmine, and Caiden.

Thank you to my surrogate moms and dads, sister-moms, brother-dads, and a host of amazing friends and human-beings who gave of time and love to be a comfort and guide throughout my life. Thank you Carol Stevens and Gerry Stevens, Christine Pierre, Dr. Joan Gillece, Suzanne Sege, Michele Lynberg and Robert Black, Brandon Wallace, Esq., Tommy Slack, Anne Seymour, Melvin

Andrews, Kelsey E. Collie, Tony Martin, Cally O'Mally, Pamela Alexander, Michael T. Mauldin and Ashia Duprey, Julie McMillan, Josephine Jackson, Melanie Campbell, Tonya Tyson, Irene Shields, Wayne Lockett, Florence Proctor, Joye Frost, Malik Washington, Tyler King, Karen Kellibrew, Cathy and Michael Costanzo, Demmette Guidry and CRUZ the Dame, Lucy and Abdus Raoof, Pat Williams, Ervin Williams, Alecia Velma Jackson, Charles C. Christian, Kevin Christian, Jeremy McShan, Kelle Masten Raul Almazar, Dr. Brian Sims, Kimberly Walsh, Demond Vega Pancho, Linda Reed, Linda Barnes, Greg Walker, Talania Foster, Antonio and Chantel Jones, Benjamin Jones, Shameer Loper and Nicholette Mohabeer, Eric Broussard Bueno and Shannon Lynberg, Bernard Marion Grayson, Jr., Selvon Waldron, Patricia Ofori, Joshua Lopez, Mitru Ciarlante, Shawn Harrison, Kellie Jackson, Naeemah Staggs, Leigh Powell, Marlon Hargraves, Peggy Williams, William Ridley, David Watson, David Calhoun, Eric Sanders, Tyrone Jordan, Bruce Faison, Mohammed Kamara, Eric Gilliam, Dr. Clemmie Solomon, Dr. William and Mrs. Pollard, Congressman John Lewis, Jacob Gillison, Rachika Prabhu, Dawn Harrell, Filiz Odabas-Geldiay, Robin Cook Jones, Emma Jean Coates, Myles "Rev Slim" Forest, Wanakhavi Wakhisi, Wilfred Lewis, Lucius Thompson, Tim Harrison, Clarence Davis, Barbara Harvey, Herman Millholand, Kevin Allen, Florence Proctor, Dr. Letitia Dzirasa, Reverend Robert Childs, Susie Stevens, Everett Williams, Alphonso Mayo, Michael Hardaway, Mitch Brooks, Alex Tremble, Olivia Farrow, Mary Beth Haller, Esq. after Alex Tremble Zeke Cohen, Dr. Kyla Liggett-Creel, Anne Coy, Dr. Jamar and Jeanette Smith, Mark Mason, and Denielle Randall. If I left a name off, please charge it to my mind and not my heart.

Thank you to our amazing publisher, Racquel Brown Gaston. You stood in the gap to get this project done.

Thank you, Juan Roberts, for taking on this project and turning it into visual work of art.

Finally, thank you Mom, Dad, and Tony. I shall continue to be a voice for the voiceless because of your sacrifice.

DEDICATION

Your love, compassion, and resilience has held our family together.

Delores Rose Short at age 88, Washington, D.C., 2022.
Photo: John Millington

AUTHOR'S NOTE

When I began the journey of writing this book, I was age 15. As an enthusiastic and confused teenager with little outlook on the process of writing and where it would take me, the project stalled for 27 years. Finally, with direction and encouragement from my family, close friends, and many who have seen me speak expressed to me, "If you had a book, I would read it," so I worked with my team over the past seven years to press forward. Well, here it is – my first published work of art – Resilient Rose – a memoir about the rebirth of dignity.

This memoir focused on many difficult and triumphant aspects of my life so please consider that it was not written to be a comprehensive account of my life – meaning – there is much left to share. These stories of my life are being prepared for another book, one that I am keen on writing in the future. One book at a time though.

The hugest internal battle for me was thinking about the readers. Would they be harmed by the traumatic details of my life's tragedies? Would they be able to read, connect, and grow through exposure to my daily triumphs? Would they judge me for what I wrote in speaking my truth? Will they appreciate my truth? How can I support readers on their own journeys of healing through my writing and speaking?

These are just some of the questions that kept me up at night and pondering during the day. I decided that telling my story was a key piece of my healing journey and hope for a better future for me, my family, and for whomever my story resonates. So, one of the things I thought was important was to provide some resources based on many of the themes covered in the pages of this book. You will find these resources in the Resource section at the back of the book on page 128. While I do not endorse these resources for personal gain, I have invited you to consider them for yourself and others in light of potentially difficult conversations. It is my way of letting you know that I care.

Thank you for investing your time, energy, and spirit in my ongoing journey of healing and recovery from trauma. I hope to meet you one day and hear your thoughts as you have trusted me with my thoughts.

INTRODUCTION

"*This* is Maggie from the vice president's office," was the voice on the other end of the phone call.

The young man was baffled as to which sort of trouble he had found himself in this time. After all, he had been in so many during other times in his life. The only other option was that this was a strange prank call. He was at his desk working feverishly to continue to promote social equality, economic justice, and civic engagement for many communities around the world.

"Which vice president?" he retorted.

"The vice president of the United States."

He froze. This was not a prank call. *Why would Vice President Biden's Office have a reason to call me?*

"The vice president," Maggie continued, "has identified local leaders across the country who have worked hard against domestic violence and sexual assault, and he would like to recognize you at the White House for your work and service."

How could this be? Advocating against domestic violence and sexual assault come so effortless to me. Why would I be recognized?

Like autopilot, the young man called his grandmother and

told her of the news. She had never been to the White House, never had a desire to visit it or any city or national landmarks here in Washington, D.C. Given the wounds both created and exposed from her childhood during the Great Depression in the 1930's and the Civil Rights Movement in the 1960s, she did not feel as if there was a place for her at such places. She did not feel as if she was an accepted part of the American story and thus felt as if her presence would have been unwelcomed. Her walk down memory lane in the nation's capital city was not always so pleasant. She was, however, ecstatic for her grandson. He shared the news with his colleagues and a few others but did not waste any time in keeping his eyes on work that day.

The day of the ceremony was overwhelming. That morning, prior to his recognition at the White House, he was scheduled to deliver the keynote address at Great Hall in honor of October's National Domestic Violence Awareness Month, hosted by the United States Department of Justice's Office on Violence Against Women. Great Hall in all its glory, stood two stories tall with Art Deco light fixtures and a 20-panel mural by Maurice Sterne. The event had been called off the previous year with the President of the United States' hosting his own event in the East Room at the White House in which he was invited and attended. So, this was a huge honor. The last person to have spoken at Great Hall was first lady Michelle Obama. He thought, who am I to follow behind her? How was this honor bestowed upon me? Nevertheless, with grace and humility, he gave his address. Delivering his message on the national stage was surreal. On stage with him was James Cole, Deputy U.S. Attorney General; Judge Susan Carbon, director for the Office on Violence Against Women and another esteemed speaker. In the audience sat his childhood therapist and his former middle school assistant principal and others all cheering for him.

The moment for the hour at the White House was

approaching. The young man graciously accepted a ride from Judge Carbon and her team. The line, not surprisingly, at the White House's State Avenue entrance was long. He prepared to take what he thought was his place at the back. Surprisingly, he was instead whisked away directly to the front. Few moments later, the young man– the guest of honor – being recognized by the White House, was in the Eisenhower Auditorium awaiting to be recognized. The Eisenhower Auditorium was located in the Executive Office Building on the grounds of the White House and was the venue where many presidents and cabinet members held major events. This office building was also home to many offices belonging to the United States President's staff. The young man had been to this auditorium many times for White House conferences and special meetings. This night, however, was different. In this audience, where he sat many times, now sat his grandmother, close friends and others celebrating the moment.

As this young man, among the 13 other recipients being recognized at the October 2011's White House Champion of Change Ceremony nervously took center stage, he was flabbergasted as to how one voice—his voice, became a voice that changed and continued to change his nation and the world. Somehow, someway, among the many sheroes and heroes nominated, he was among the chosen few. But how could this be, when only a few years ago, at age 13, he decided that life was too painful to live? Despite his future strapped on his back, two bus tokens, and the comfort of the $5 lunch money his grandmother gave him daily, he found his way to the neighborhood bridge at North Capitol Street and Rhode Island Avenue, as the only way to ease his pain was to jump to his death.

PART I
Reckoning

This is the only known photo of William at age 3,
Washington, D.C.,
Photo credit: Family archives

HUMDINGER

The live club scene being depicted on the square legged box with black and white images escaping from it, was just another usual Saturday night programming.

Grown folks packed together like sardines, sweated and gyrated on the dance floor as the music pounded the room. Various colors of the rainbow swept across the air in quick flashes and folks drunk from the music became lost in a trance. It was just another night until a 5 feet 4, light-skinned, red-boned firecracker became the anecdote for many in the trance as all eyes were on her.

Shocked and rattled at the image of her teenage daughter-my mom Jacqueline--protruding from the square legged box, the feisty, hot-tempered Rose Delores Short-- now self-named Delores Rose Short, in the hopes that Rose would never again be uttered—and who we affectionately called Mama, immediately marched her petite lean figure to the club owner to make a few things clear.

"If I see my daughter down here again, Imma call da police. She ain't but 15 years old."

Mama knew that threatening the club owner was not going to have any effect upon her daughter, but it was another territorial war to be won. The 15-year-old dainty and feminine humdinger, with the infectious smile and hypnotic laugh was not going to be stopped by anyone, period. At family events, when Mom entered the room, it was lights—camera—action. She stole the show. She was going to be noticed and that was a requirement. She loved to party. She loved to dance. Dancing was therapy. She was known to slap men in the dark, if they attempted to touch her while she gave them a dance treat. She loved men with a pep in their step and was not shy with the women either. The uncontrollable, rebellious, party girl Jackie, to whom Mama rarely showed affection, as she probably was not capable, was the oldest and only girl of four children.

Mama oftentimes told us stories of Mom.

"That girl was beyond control. She hated school."

Mama, however, was not beyond popping Mom's mouth when she talked back, nor taking the belt to her rear end. At times, Mama would even communicate with that sacred African American language, no doubt inherited from the Motherland, where some words are spoken without a sound, but rather with "the look"— where pleasantries hastily dash away to seek a hiding place and sternness takes center place. That language is known to have sent shivers down many spines.

Mama was not the only one who was at war with this young woman. According to Mama, school could not tame Mom. She would hand them hell on a platter. Her school skipping and hopping days caused the truancy police to make her a guest in their transport vehicle constantly. Even for nearly a year, her address was changed to a detention center. Mom's temporary absence from high school became a permanent one.

Mom was heading down a track that was Mama's own worst nightmare. There was no need for her only daughter, over whom she was very protective, to repeat the story once lived and told. The high school girl who became pregnant in the 1950s by a physically, verbally and emotionally abusive man, a decade her senior, and ran away to Baltimore, Maryland, with him. She desperately sought independence from her family in Washington, D.C. This new taste of freedom dazzled and enticed her, but it came at a silent cost. The literal fight for Mama's life was a daily occurrence. Mama left that world behind when her boyfriend, Mitch Jones, frustrated by the constant crying of their three months old daughter, slapped a newborn Jackie.

Waiting for Mitch to go to work, Mama reached out once more to her family in Washington, D.C. to rescue her. With a pot of beans still simmering on the stove, Mama quickly grabbed her daughter's essentials and fled. Mitch was not far behind, but Mama never looked back. Returning to Washington, D.C. from Baltimore was supposed to bring Mama relief. Perhaps, it did, but it brought a different kind of pain.

Fifteen years later, the story repeated itself. Mom and her flamboyant dance partner took their partnership to another level. Perhaps it was because Mom did not get much affection from Mama. Perhaps it was because the most shielded woman the party girl has ever known was the one who gave birth to her. Perhaps, she partied much, for in that moment, she abandoned the cares of her world. Whatever the reason, it brought my brother Rodney into existence to a teenage mom. Experience-none. Maturity-none. Responsibility-much. The struggle began for the child to raise a child. The additional burden for a grandmother in an already tense household multiplied. The year was 1969.

Two years later after Rodney came Anthony, affectionately known as Tony. He carried neither the DNA of a flamboyant dance partner. Two years after Tony, I came busting in the world, as William, named after my dad, William Kellibrew. In and out of prison my dad went. My sister, Manyka, whom we nicknamed, "Nicci," followed two years later in 1976, and then my youngest brother, Da'Vone, two years after that.

Instability was centerfold in our lives. Around four years

old, we moved in with Mama and her husband, Mr. Mark Short, who resided in an apartment complex on D Street, Southeast, Washington, D.C. The three-bedroom apartment did not give way to house an additional seven people, so bedtime meant bodies would not be necessarily found in beds or bedrooms, but any place a body could lie.

I attended Harris Elementary School where I saw my first helicopter land in the school field and where I learned how to sing Lift Every Voice and Sing and was introduced to this concept called harmony. My time at Harris would soon come to an end. At six years old, when I was in the first grade, we moved to King Square Apartments in Landover, Maryland. My dad moved to a prison complex I heard folks called the Big House. And our home became the dwelling place of Lorraine, Mom's new affection.

THE HOLY BED

Lorraine was nothing short of exceptional, genuine, loyal, kind, and soft-spoken. Freckles and moles decorated her cocoa brown face. She was scrawny, and no more than 110 pounds, but taller than Mom. When I met her family, I could not have helped but believe that she was considered one of the family's outcasts. Perhaps it was because unlike her other sisters who fashioned dresses and fancy flats, Lorraine sported jean pants and loafers. Her short red strands needed only to be brushed.

In our home, she found her place. She took a special interest in me. Lorraine and I would often share a book on our living room couch. Even though I stumbled to bring meaning to jumbled letters on the pages, she patiently coached me through. Lorraine was nice to me. She did not show as much attention to my other brothers and sister as she did me. She cared about us all. She taught me how to tie my tennis shoes. She even taught me that a Hollywood actor was the President of the United States. She said his name was Ronald Reagan.

Although I was attending yet another new school, Dodge Park Elementary, Lorraine's college classroom became mine as well.

For Lorraine, the college student who majored in visual arts, promoting education was effortless. It was no wonder that she took me to her painting classes in college. I also frequented Manny, her sugar daddy's, workplace, an auto-supply store, on Rhode Island Avenue, just across the D.C. border line. He weighed over 200 pounds and stood over six feet and was always kind and giving. Lorraine always received a few dollars here and there and shared a little with me. I kept silent and observed more than I spoke.

Like we normally do, we moved again, this time to Dodge View Apartments in Landover, Maryland. Lorraine joined us. She played her role as the other guardian. But, again, I did not have a clue as to her official role. It was the time of year for falling leaves, turkey, stuffing, cranberry sauce, sweet potato pies, chocolate and red velvet cakes, eggnog, macaroni and cheese, fried chicken, and homemade biscuits and family. We were all gearing up to have dinner around the family table. The responsibility of having a public conversation with the Lord about the meal he provided had landed on my shoulders. Lorraine took me to one of the bedrooms. The bed upon which I sat was no longer an ordinary bed; it was *holy*.

> *"Repeat after me," she commanded softly.*
> *"Thank you God," she began.*
> *"Thank you God. "*
> *"For our food..."*
> *"For our food... "*
> *"For nourishing our bodies..."*
> *"For nourishing our bodies..."*
> *"Amen."*
> *"Amen."*

After I repeated it to memory, Lorraine continued.

"Now put your hands together, close your eyes, bow your head, and say it by yourself." I now knew how to pray. Sitting at the head of the table, I did as the nurturer-my home professor—had instructed me. I still recite those words today.

Though Lorraine was doing a good job at being a role model when Dad again went to stay for a while at the Big House, I missed the long walks, rides on his back, ride on his shoulders, the comparison of the back in the days versus nowadays music, and the soother personality that tended to be a buffer against Mom's. That feeling of being protected by my own superman was unmatched. Oh, how I longed for his letters to us! No matter the physical distance, of choice against the enemy of separation. It was no surprise that when he came home from the Big House, he wanted Lorraine gone from the house. All three of them-my mother, Lorraine, and my dad would argue constantly about it. Lorraine was right in the middle of it. They would call each other names that were only reserved for people one did not like and sometimes it would get physical, putting it lightly.

The ordinary bed that had become holy was now the sight of a wretched transformation. "I know this is going to be a hard question for you to answer, but do you want me or your father to live here with you?" Lorraine asked me directly.

I preferred the holy bed. Lorraine's question was by far the toughest I had to answer. I felt trapped in the middle. I felt like everything landed on my shoulders and I could not get it off. I was afraid to answer the question and stalled for a long time. My father was in the next room waiting for Lorraine to come out. This was killing me inside. I thought about everything that Lorraine was teaching me and how I loved it and wanted to learn more. She was a wealth of knowledge, and I did not know how to get my father to understand that she was a good person. I was hoping that they all would just settle down and all live together, but that was impossible. So, eventually my father moved in and Lorraine moved out.

"Oh, how I longed for his letters to us!"

CHANGES

The mornings at Dodge View were quite busy with all us children around. It was quite noisy and full of energy. It was fun. I was active around the neighborhood. I started collecting Matchbox and Hot Wheels cars. I would make roads in the dirt and act like I was playing with the cars in a city all my own.

I was also glad not to move to another school. I was starting to get to know the kids at Dodge Park Elementary School, though I had a hard time getting along sometimes in class. As always, it was as if my mouth was that of a parrot in the wild—always producing sounds. Those sounds of chatter did not get me any closer access to the inner circle of those who defined cool. It was just another arena of me standing outside a ring looking at everyone else inside of it.

I would often be late for class because my household made it a point to be the poster family for what we as African Americans called "CP" time, referring to "colored people time." Growing up, I always heard stories and saw people react to those in my culture showing up way after the time scheduled to be at a place. Adults joked about it and if they wanted an event to start at a certain time, they would have actually given folks a time about two hours earlier than the real time. Some would even jokingly ask if the time, "CP time" was real time. I do not think this "CP time" was true for every family in my culture, but I know my family mastered it. I was constantly embarrassed and ashamed when I arrived at school during this "CP" time. I would feel the negative attention attach itself to me. I eventually adopted the term, "certain people's time."

Mom was multi-talented. She danced, sang and was a great roller-skater too. Also, Mom was an avid swimmer, so we learned how to swim. She loved seafood. There were days when she purchased so much shrimp and crabs and we would just chow down. We would eat right in the living room, often preparing for a much anticipated Washington Redskins versus Dallas Cowboys game. This usually happened at the first of the month directly after Mom received her food stamps. Down to the D.C. Wharf we went.

When my father wanted to be great, he was. He protected me from my mother's beatings and when I say beatings, I mean beatings. Rodney got it the worst though. She would beat him unmercifully and would not spare anything. She would beat all of us with anything upon which she could get her hands: a broom stick, a mop handle, a belt, anything she could grab in her reach. Unbeknownst to me, I thought everyone grew up this way.

Unfortunate events continued to lurk at Dodge View. I had developed a liking to fire. I would light cardboard boxes and kids would watch and we would all run away from the burning boxes. It therefore did not come as a surprise that I was blamed for a huge fire in an apartment building down the road. I was sitting in front of my apartment building, and I could hear the fire engines screaming in the background and the sound of emergency vehicles closing in on our apartment complex. I decided to go and play with my Matchbox and Hot Wheels toy cars making new roads in the dirt, drawing out my miniature city. Neighbors, firemen and police officers approached me from behind.

"Son, where do you live? Where are your parents?"

I took them to my apartment and led them to my father. They asked me in front of my father if I had anything to do with the fire and I answered truthfully.

"No!"

I really did not do it this time. After the fire-fighters and police left, my father took me into the room and asked me again.

"You can tell me, did you set that apartment on fire?"

And I once again replied with a truthful, but scary, "No." From that point on, I did not want to see a match. I had learned my lesson very well.

I took that lesson with me when we then moved away from the apartment and to the big white house on the hill. Vine Street, off Southern Avenue in Maryland, three blocks from the D.C. border, was a three-story mansion. I mean it had not one, not two, not three, not four but five bedrooms! Wow! What was a kid to do? It also had all these little spaces for me to hide from my imaginary friends, my real friends and for my siblings and I to hide from each other. It was so cool. There were so many hideouts, I wondered if I had ever discovered all of them. Did I mention we even had a basement, an attic, a kitchen, and living room so big, our old apartment could fit in them? Even the back yard had a whole lot of space for my brothers to build their basketball court with the natural material of dirt.

We were bonafide Americans now with our white picket fence and neighbors with strange accents. The strange accent belonged to the mother of the two boys who became my friends. It was bizarre because my third-grade mind simply could not figure out what nationality or ethnic background they represented, and I wondered if everyone from their country looked like them and spoke Spanish too. They were not black, not white, but they looked white. Nonetheless, one of those "looked white" kids became my best friend. They must have had something similar to the unspoken African American language because every time we were playing outside and their mom would come, something invisible would pick up their legs and they would be gone like the wind.

Vine Street brought with it other adventures. There was the swing set in the yard directly across the street of the old man that lived a life with his granddaughter that pre-dated Thomas Edison. I could not have imagined not being able to say let there be light and then having no switch to make that light appear. Well, though people mocked and laughed at the old man and his granddaughter, they taught me a vital lesson--perhaps that switch was not a big deal in the grand scheme of things because I was happy on their swing in their backyard that had no light and sometimes unhappy in my big ole mansion that had plenty of switches.

On the other hand, other situations were no laughing matter for another set of neighbors. They had two children who I learned were theirs, but not theirs. What does that mean, I asked? Well, they were theirs because something happened with their momma and poppa or siblings or grandparents where the government gave them a new family to keep them safe. The problem is they kept having new families. I was thankful for the consistency of my old family.

Some things from my *old family* did move with us when we came to Vine Street—Lorraine and Mom's temper. Dad moved away again to the Big House for a shorter time period. For all that Lorraine did, Mom was not as equally kind. One day she hit Lorraine so hard with a bat that Lorraine's right wrist went immediately limp and then dangled. Lorraine did not fight back. Her arm did get the company of a brace. Another day, Mom took her fighting words to four men in front of the house. "Leave her alone! Leave her alone!" I repeated. One retrieved a car jack like tool and applied it to Mom's head as if it was a ball and the tool was a bat. Mom could not fight back. She lay there while the men jumped in their cars and sped away. Few days later, she came back from the hospital with her neck having had the company of a brace. I sat by her side and gave her as much comfort as a third grader could give.

When I was not comforting Mom, I was comforting myself. I would make these trips to the "ice cream parlor" that required a special set of skills found with an intelligence field agent.

First, it was nightfall. Second, I would climb a fence. Then I would creep without so much of a sound, not even a mouse would have noticed me. I would ease my way through my neighbors' basement window that I had left open from earlier times in anticipation of my return. The creaks from the floor above me, from the house's occupants going about their nightly business, would cause me to hold my heart to prevent it from leaping outside my body. Still, my desire for my greatest love that came in all flavors-vanilla, chocolate, strawberry, butter pecan would have me get to them at all costs. I was even considerate of its true owner, so I would bring my own spoon. I did not know what was making my heart dance louder—the fear of being caught in a trap like a mouse or the excitement in feeling those cold juicy sensations dissolve in my mouth. Flavor by flavor, my spoon made its rounds. There were no blank stares at an empty space in a freezer where ice cream was to occupy but did not because lack of money dictated otherwise. There was no Nicci do you want some or Rodney do you want some? None of that. It was just William. I was in bliss. As the taste took hold of me, giving into my delight, my alert system kept signaling-that was enough, we gotta get out of here. I needed to have enough to say my clandestine trip was worth it, but I could not have enough to cause suspicion. So, after I finished my balancing act, I transformed back into a spy and snuck out the window without being heard. I crawled my way to the fence and without so much of a sound climb back over. Just like that, I was gone. I was gone again night after night after night, and some days too.

Just like I was gone like the wind from the ice cream parlor, the school bus was gone like the wind from us many mornings. Walking miles to school, hence, being late became a permanent fixture in our lives. The nomadic lifestyle continued in fourth grade when I moved to Doswell E. Brooks Elementary School.

Next, came the move that would change our lives forever. I was in the fifth grade, and moved to Gunther Street in Capitol Heights, Maryland. Dad had moved out to his own apartment with his new girlfriend, Jess; but unlike custom, he was not the force that caused Lorraine to flee this time. She once again became the past tense in our lives, and so did another thing we valued most.

> *"Next, came the move that would change our lives forever."*

THE BULLY

On your mark. I sat in the front of the school bus, at the edge of my seat, anxiously awaiting my next move. *Get set.* I placed my feet behind the white line waiting to sprint off at any second. *Go.* The very instant I heard screeching doors moved open, I dashed off my feet and sprinted out. Like Flash Gordon, I was gone. James, the bully, who was usually trained in his huge yard by his dad to be the next Rocky Balboa was not going to catch me. That was not a sparring match in which I was about to participate, with James, two years my senior. I was the same guy who taunted, teased and mimicked him quite frequently during his training, and everyone in the neighborhood knew it. In fact, as embarrassing as it was to walk into class no earlier than 10 a.m. most mornings, with Nicci and Da'Vone, I would continuously take the scenic, adventurous, and scary route through the woods for many miles. I would do so just to avoid the bully. I refused to catch the school bus so I would avoid facing its regular passenger, James. My goal was to stay elusive and alive. As such, we developed a cat and mouse relationship.

One day, my brothers had had enough of my being on the run. Tony and Rodney demanded that I toughen up in more ways than one. My brother Tony would smack me so often upside my head that even at the sight of this dark, towering, 12-year-old, basketball frame; I would flinch, as if a knee jerk reaction.

"Toughen up Chump," always followed.

Tony taunted me to fight him in preparation for me to stand up for myself. I was not a fighter. But, if I were not willing to fight Tony, my biggest bully, why would I fight Rocky Balboa? The truth is though I had no desire to fight Balboa, I feared him. Not everyone in the neighborhood was the subject of my fear. Older kids, including my brothers, would make fun of the way I talked and walked. I had a switch like Mom to which I was unaware, especially when I wore flip flops. Unlike the older kids, the younger kids would follow me around as I was simply jovial, light spirited and always playful. So much so, I frequently stayed up late at night. Perhaps subconsciously, I knew it would be an added factor in missing the school bus.

I sprinted off the bus straight into Mom's kitchen, as routine. I was a mama's boy and everyone knew it. I helped her with cooking as I usually did, but this time, something was different.

"Bam-Bam," as my mom referred to me, "grab me the butter out the fridge and the rolling pin for this dough."

Though she appreciated her sous chef, she knew that I preferred playing outside over cooking. On one of my sprinting days, Rodney walked in and told her that I was running from James.

Mom's head spun around like the character in The Exorcist, "get back out dere and fight back! Pick up the closest thing to you. Kick! Bite! Fight for your life. Get outta here!"

The inevitable was here. I had to face James or face Mom. The news spread like wildfire that day. The promotion began for the fight of the century. James and all the neighborhood kids waited just a block away beyond the horizon. Cheers and screams filled the air as my brothers and I approached. This fight stole the gambling spotlight from the usual dice games on Nova Avenue, upon which teenagers placed their bets. There was no turning back now. Ding…Ding…Ding! The bell rang in my head. James and I took our places in the center of a circle of rowdy kids. We proceeded with some sort of circular footwork and took jabs at each other. Round and around we went. I aimed to avoid the sting of the Balboa punch, mostly. Balboa swung again. Missing his punch by inches, I fell on the ground and my head barely missed the curb. Before I knew it, my worst nightmare was on top of me. James was pounding my head. I panicked. I quickly saw a way out as his chest was exposed. Pick up the closest thing to you. Kick! Bite! Fight for your life. Like a Sub-Saharan African Nile crocodile, I slammed my jaws shut into his chest. I held on and did not let go. He screamed and screamed. An eternity had passed. I finally retracted my jaws. He scurried away from the arena and dashed home.

I could not believe it. The underdog was titled the champion. I was the Rocky Balboa after all. The cheers came from everywhere. In bliss, I giddily made my way down the street, celebrating the moment. I turned onto Gunther Street and unexpectedly ran into Mom, who was heading to the fight.

"Come ere!" Mom angrily shouted.

I was bewildered by her outrage. I hurriedly advanced.

Smack! I felt the sting from a heavy open hand across my face. With no warning, Mom had slapped me so hard. She assumed given my predisposition prior to the fight, I had lost. The good news had not reached her.

"No! No! No! He won! He won the fight!" my brothers yelled.

"Good. You learned your lesson. Next time don't run from nobody," Mom retorted.

Later, we were all sitting on the stairs, and we heard a knock on the door.

"Get da door Bam-Bam," Mom instructed.

Standing beyond the threshold of our front door, stood James and his dad, with the moonlight in the backdrop. Everyone's jaws dropped. James's dad proceeded to address Mom.

"I had to take my son to the hospital for a bite mark caused by your son."

"Well, don't have your kid fight my kid. Make sure he stays away." She slammed the door. That was the end of James, the bully.

DEBONAIRE

Days passed. Still no mom. As the oldest, Rodney became the default parent. My younger sister Nicci and I were sitting at our usual hangout spot—the steps next to the front door. We heard chatter outside, followed by the clicking and clacking of the door. Unsurprisingly, the motion of the door becoming ajar immediately followed.

Suddenly, I came to a halt. I was in complete awe. My eyes elevated my sight to who I thought was the most immaculate man on earth. I was nine. Even then, I knew a debonair when I saw one. Nicci was not as surprised since she had met this man sometime before. He was about 6 feet tall, muscle defined, lean, with a caramel complexion. His hair was black, thin, and slicked back. He was clean cut, with light brown, deep eyes. It was as if he was magic. Poof— came out of nowhere.

And this debonair, who was my mom's friend, instantly earned the approval of my sister and me. He did not come to us with candy, or sugary items like most adults. He raised the bar and introduced himself to us with a handful of coins. We were simply beyond ourselves. This was like Christmas. Being on welfare limited us mostly to items purchasable with food stamps. We quickly ran to the store and converted our cash prize into sugary items. Marcus impressed us very much.

He did a lot of things with my mom and us six kids. We were quickly becoming a family. As he had a car, he took us skating and to the movies frequently. He also played tug of war with us and would always win with him and Mom on one side of the rope, and us kids on the other. Whenever my dad and his new girlfriend, Jess came to visit, he and Marcus would play chess. My mom and Jess sat on the guys' laps. All seemed to have been going well.

One day Mom had all six of us form a line next to each other. Rodney the oldest, was 15, Tony 12, Cody, Mama's son, who lived with us was also 12. Nicci, the only girl was 7, Da'Vone 5 and I was the middle child at 9. We were in trouble. The drill sergeant sat on Marcus' lap. She got up and paced back and forth. I knew the beatings would have followed shortly. The 5-foot-four sergeant towered over me. She simply raised her hand and I started crying and slowly wet my pants. As punishment, though I required a stool upon which to stand, my mom made me wash all the dishes. That was one sort of punishment for which I was grateful, as it was my opportunity to escape the other room with all the merciless beatings that were about to take place. Memories flooded me.

"Who the f%*# left these dishes in the sink! Everybody, get the f%*# up!" My mom's yelling from the kitchen awoke us one night. She and Marcus had just arrived home from one of their many mysterious late nights out.

Before I was able to get my bearings, I saw my door flung open; and Marcus, with full throttle, stormed into my bedroom with the black hose from the washing machine, and whacked me across my chest, back and legs. This was my first beating from Marcus. I was forced to the kitchen and made to wash the dishes immediately. This way of life was harsh to bear.

As I climbed the stool, my heart broke for those in the

line-up in the other room. My oldest brother and my sister always received the worst beatings. I specifically remembered a beating episode with my sister months earlier. I vividly recalled my mom instructing her to not wear high water pants to school. We had just come from school and the plan was to have her sneak into her room, while I distracted Mom. I attended to Mom inside her bedroom while she watched television. As my sister snuck by, something caught my mom's attention. She took a second glance in my sister's direction and her face curled. My sister was now out of view. My attempt to distract Mom had failed.

"Ummm come here?" She called out to my sister.

"I said. Come. Ere!" Mom continued. Nicci slowly appeared.

"Didn't I tell you not to wear those pants to school?" Silence gripped the air. "Take off your clothes. You are going to get it."

I sat on the top of the stairs and watched as my mom broke a glass ketchup bottle and broom on my sister. I counted the number of items my mom used to beat my sister that day. The number was seven, including a mop, an extension cord, and a belt. I cried and cried, in hopes that my mom would stop. I do not know what possessed Nicci to be disobedient. I knew it wasn't Nicci's fault. My mom was the same woman who had flung her against our living room wall when she reported to our grandmother, our mom's stealing habits from Mama's purse. It was the same mom who threw utensils at my head and when I dodged, she asked me to reposition my head, and then threw a chair at it. Fortunately, I dodged again. These are just some of the experiences from which I based my fear for those in the line-up. Washing dishes was a welcome escape, but a very guilty one.

Like a romance, the beginning stages of our relationship with Marcus started to fade. He started to control what my mom ate and what we ate. One morning, Mom and Marcus gathered us at the breakfast table for our usual Kellogg's cornflakes. Marcus geared our attention to the nutrients on the box and inquired of us to tell him the meaning of a word he had chosen. We were clueless as to the answer.

With no response, Marcus proceeded to assist us with the definition.

"Hog-shit," he enlightened us.

Everyone immediately dropped the spoon. That was the last day I ate cornflakes. Some days Mom would just stay out late, and food may or may not have been in the house. I did not mind her staying out as long as we had food in the house. If not, I would go to my best friend, Harry's house and I would eat there. One day while my mom was home, I heard her scream from her bedroom in despair.

"Let me go! Help me!"

I jumped up from the kitchen table and I rushed to her bedroom. Standing at the threshold of the door, I saw Mom trying to escape Marcus' grip. Her screams were piercing. I ran downstairs to get help from my brothers. When we returned to Mom's bedroom, they had both reached the door and Marcus was trying to shut it while pushing her back. She was his hostage. He controlled her every move, including her goings and comings.

Mom's absence from home was ever increasing. Some days, Mom would simply be missing. Marcus did not like my grandmother, Mama, who was Mom's strongest advocate. Seeing my grandmother as a threat, he forced Mom to take out a restraining order against her own mother, preventing her from coming near our home. As such, when Mama wanted to deliver groceries or a few boxes of Popeye's chicken to us, she had to do so from the corner where we would meet her.

One day, Mom's dad, granddad Mitch, and Mom's brothers were at the house and Mom was not there. Marcus had held her hostage at the top of a hill with Rodney in the back of the car and Mom in the passenger seat. I remembered going up the street by myself delivering messages back and forth, until eventually, he released her. Mom tried to get out of the relationship. She eventually went on the run trying to get away from the debonair who had transformed into something unrefined.

I was in my mom's room with my granddad's wife, Ms. Sally. Mom lifted up her shirt to show Ms. Sally something. And to my horror, it was a revelation. I did not know what I was looking for. I became instantly bewildered. I saw what appeared to be purple, black and blue shaded areas. Marcus had pummeled upon my mom's body. It took me back to one of my earliest memories at about 4 years old.

It was the heart of the 70's, Southeast D.C.—upbeat music and for some, a carefree attitude. Like many nights, we had plenty of visitors and card playing was in full swing. As hypnotized as the card players and the good time rollers were, that was about to come to an end. I thought. Thump, thump, thump, were the sounds of feet urgently running down the set of steps in the hallway outside of our apartment. My curiosity piqued. What was happening? Why were there screams accompanying the thumps? In no time at all, my answer busted into our apartment. I was stunned. A man was pounding on my mom's friend, who happened to be my cousin's mother. This man beat her into our apartment. He beat her all the way to the sofa. He continued to beat her on the sofa. I looked around. To my dismay, the card players and good time rollers remained in full swing. Didn't they hear her? Didn't they see her? Why has her cry fallen on deaf ears? Maybe beating a woman as if she were a punching bag was deemed as normal an activity for those playing cards in the same room? I was baffled. I was 4 and something did not feel right just like it did not feel right about Marcus, now at age 9. Was I the only one to know this?

I looked at my mom's purple, black and blue shaded areas. Did Ms. Sally really see them? Did she really hear Mom's unspoken cries? Will her cries go on deaf ears? Life has become full circle, again, with me just standing there, aghast. My mom did not want granddad to know. She made sure that Mama did not know. Who would have thought that what was about to unfold would have changed our lives forever?

"*I could still feel his breath upon me, though there was a wall between us.*"

SILENCE

It was a hot summer day outside and a cold winter morning inside. The day was Monday, July 2, 1984. The sun gently slapped my face, greeting me. I blinked my way to full consciousness. As my blinking simmered and my eyes became fully widened, I heard piercing screams, almost unbearable, coming from a distance outside of our home. Life rose up in me, and I sprung.

I did not know who else, besides myself, was home. I quickly whisked cold from my eyes and arose from the bed. The screams, however, became louder and louder as I approached our living room.

"Call the police! Call the police!"

Wait. I knew these screams. I knew them because I had heard them several times before. I made my way over to the window to see what was happening.

"Call the police! Call the police," Mom kept yelling.

Marcus had shackled her wrist with his palms and was dragging her towards our house. Tony, who was on the verge of his 13th birthday, had fastened himself onto her waist. As Marcus dragged Mom in one direction, she screamed, and Tony with all his might tried to pull her in the opposite direction. Like some kids on a playground, some of Mom's neighbors, the powerless and bystanders alike, stood at a distance similar to the night of card playing and beating.

Perhaps, I believed I too was powerless. I switched my attention from my mom's screams to the growls in my stomach. I attended to my famished pain and headed upstairs to the kitchen. I opened the refrigerator, and it reminded me of the temperature of a cooled oven. I flipped on the switch in the kitchen to see if everything else was okay. The non-illuminated bulbs addressed my inquiry. Thank goodness for the beams from the morning sun to light my way around the kitchen. With very little choice, I descended back to the first floor. My feet tightly gripped the carpet that layered each step. I opened the side door curiously, and Mom was sitting down in the grass exhausted. To her right was Tony, and her left, Marcus. With soundless movements, I slowly closed the door and locked it.

I got a hold of my Matchbox and Hot Wheels cars and began to play with them. With every play, I grew a distance away from reality. I did not get far into my delightful imaginary world when bursts of thumper on the door brought me back to the present. I leapt to the window and saw Mom frantically banging on the door.

I opened it and I felt the wind she left behind as she dashed to the living room window pleading to the spectators, "Call the police! Call the police!" Mom repeated her rallying cry. Tony had now made his way to a wall in the living room. Marcus, now the ex-boy-friend, was facing me, but had his back to his ex-girlfriend and her 12-year-old son. His subsequent actions caused fear to paralyze me. He pulled out what appeared to be an inverted L shaped, black, metal structure with a small circle at the tip. He seemed to have separated parts of it somehow, then reached for his inside pocket and removed tiny cylinder-shaped objects with oval tips. He insert-ed several of them into the inverted L shape object and then, as if in a hurry, walked over to Mom. Her cries of "Call the police," became louder. She turned and faced Marcus. He pointed the inverted L shaped object in her face. As if an automatic response, her hands jumped in the air, followed by a loud sound, "No!!!" The inverted L shape object was deafened to her sounds.

"Pop! Pop!" The L shape object released sounds.

Mom did not even have time to turn around to instruct us as to what to do. Her lifeless body dropped to the floor effortlessly. Her arms sprawled out and she fell on her side. She painted the walls, the carpet and everything in her pathway, red. I felt the bottom of my stomach fall on the floor. Time had stopped. I was frozen. The first thought that entered my mind was, "I am dead." I did not know exactly where Mom went, but I knew I was soon to follow. After all, I went everywhere with Mom and she was not going to leave me now. The only difference with this trip was I had only seconds to prepare. My stomach fell and kept falling. Sweat and heart palpitations were an all-time high. Confusion flogged me. This preparation to join my mom was the scariest feeling I have ever undergone, and I longed for the moments of when I fell, or the times I received whipping for misbehaving. My eyes remained fixated on the ex-boyfriend's every move. He made his way quickly over to the 12-year-old.

Tony, still in his original position, was as quiet as a mouse. I watched my biggest bully stand there for the first time, silent. He has moved from heroism to standing alone silently. I watched Tony and waited for some guidance on how I should behave. I did not get it. Instead, in an instant, in the midst of utter despair, and the inability to think or move, or I dare say breathe, my body jolted. My heart left my body. The hair on my body cringed and stood alert. The inside of my body had ceased to work.

Marcus was not finished. He pointed the inverted L shaped black metal structure at Tony's throat and applied pressure to what appeared to be a lever. Tony fell to the ground like a leaf in autumn falling from a tree branch. His knees gripped the ground, and he hunched over like a ball. He was gasping for air. The cylin-

der-shaped object exited through the back of his neck and created
a fountain of blood sprouting up and over his head onto the carpet.
I was hypnotized by the back of his neck and as is programmed,
followed the upstream of blood from his neck onto the carpet, where
it had created puddles. The carpet could not soak up the puddles fast
enough. The painting of the room in red continued. I did not know
to which painter to give my ghastly look. Although Tony drew my
attention because of his wordless fight with every gasp, Marcus made
the decision for me.

He made his way back over to Mom, and as if she was not
already silenced; he released more of the tiny cylinder-shaped
objects into her. I knew I was next. He briskly continued his trail
to me. I tensed and braced myself for the inevitable. I knew this
was the moment I would join my mother in that unknown place.
I had given up every ounce of hope. Marcus squatted in front
of me. I saw him not only eye to eye, but also, I saw through its
circle at the tip, the dark tunnel of that inverted L shaped black
metal object. Something, as if, involuntarily, clicked. I no longer
wanted to join Mom. Without hesitation, I opened my mouth
and hastily the words flowed uninterruptedly.

"Please don't kill me! Please don't kill me! I'll do anything!"

No response. It was just the stillness from the inverted L
shape object. As if a knee jerk reaction, I lifted my head toward the
ceiling, clasped my hands together, closed my eyes and pleaded.

"God, please don't let him kill me! I'll do anything."

Moments passed by. I felt a rush of air leave my presence.
I slowly brought my head down, unclasped my hands and opened
my eyes.

"You can leave. Call the police," the executioner said in a
shallow, but a matter-of-fact tone.

"Did I hear him right?" I questioned myself. I did not want
to take any chances of asking him to repeat himself. So, after a few
moments, I revved up the energy inside of me and lifted my body

toward the door. The room was almost completely silent except for two sounds—the sounds of Tony gasping for air and Marcus' footsteps pacing the floor near Mom. I refused to make one sound. I was scared that Marcus would change his mind and release some of those cylinder- shaped objects into me as well. I stood and reached for the knob of the front door. I twisted the knob and slowly opened the door, milliseconds at a time. I put one foot through the door and looked at Marcus across the room.

"Do you want me to lock it?" I asked, still frozen in fear.

There was no response from across the room. One final look back and all I could think was, I will go get some help for you Mom and Tony. Leaving them was one of the toughest decisions I had ever made as a child. I thought I had abandoned my mom. Never in my life have I felt such pressure and urgency to get help. Knowing I had to leave them to still accomplish that was horrendous beyond words. Still, I put the other foot through the door, locked it and closed it behind me. Outside, I walked slowly past the living room window thinking that I could still get killed. Like a snail with salt poured over it, I put one foot in front of the other and forced myself to walk down the steps of our porch. Many times, I had sat on this very porch and cried because Mom refused to take me with her. I would watch the car drive away until it disappeared. Not today. I was not safe yet.

I knew the former debonair was watching. He had replaced my mom's presence at that window by standing guard over his kills. He owned that room that day, probably the most control he had in his life. I could still feel his breath upon me, though there was a wall between us. *Will I make it? Will he let me continue to walk away?* With one turn away from the window, I knew my mission. I pushed ahead through our driveway looking back at the window to make sure I was still allowed to leave. With my hot, sweat barefoot, still one foot slowly in front of the other, I made it to the end of the driveway. My world, as I knew it, had changed drastically. I was 10 years old.

" My stomach fell and kept falling. "

AFTERMATH

"*Call* the police! Call the police!"

I had transformed from the careful turtle to the desperate
cat, ready to dodge anything in my way. I sped from the driveway
as fast as my little legs could have carried me.

"Call the police! Call the police!" The same words poured
without effort.

I had no access to any more words or syllables. Mom's friend
Snookie's house seemed to have been the logical destination but
the Doberman pinscher who stood guard there thought differently.
As if the doberman's residence was not my intended venue, I back-
tracked by landing on the doorsteps of Harry's house.

Thomp! Thomp! Thomp! Each bang was quicker and
louder than the one before.

Thomp! Thomp! Thomp! My mind and heart kept racing.
The door finally responded to my call. Seeing Harry and his uncle
was like finding an oasis after wandering days in a desert. Like paramedics arriving on the scene, they attended to me. They hastily sat
me down at the kitchen table in hopes that I would be able to gather
my thoughts. I did not. My index finger immediately spotted the

telephone on the wall and as if heading to attack it, took jabs in the phone's direction.

"Call the police! Call the police! My momm...my motha...my...my!"

It was a lost cause. No more words from the English language were going to come forth. I saw Harry's uncle pick up the phone and I saw his lips moving. In what then seemed like seconds, sirens were going off and outside were fire trucks, ambulances and police officers. They took me and secured me in Harry's neighbor's house next door. The room in which I was taken had children's books and games.

"Do you want anything to eat, drink, anything at all?" they asked.

No was the word I would have said, had I remembered how to speak.

"Can you tell me what happened William?" an officer asked.

There was silence.

"Can you draw what happened inside your house?"

I did not only remember how to nod or shake my head, I remembered how to draw. With a black crayon that the officer took from the kid's desk, I drew, shakily, two stick figures lying on the floor. One was longer than the other. Then I drew another stick figure of Mom's ex-boyfriend standing up with an inverted L-shaped black object in his hand. With a red crayon, I drew a line coming from the back of Tony's neck to over his head. I colored the rest of the paper red with no boundaries. The bubbly feeling inside my stomach grew exponentially.

Nonstop sirens continued to fill the air.

"You are surrounded. Come out!" Minutes went by. The demand continued. No response. Hours went by.

"You are surrounded. Come on out!"

Guarded by the police who were eager for answers I could not provide, I thought of the rest of my family. *Where were Nicci,*

Rodney, Da'Vone, Cody, mama, my dad, uncles, everyone? I am by myself. After the cops finished with me, the owner of the house invited me into the family room for snacks and to watch television. The news about the current events outside my home flashed across the tv screen. I was still mute. I was still frozen in disbelief and what ifs.

Three hours passed. "You are surrounded. Come on out!"

"Boom! Boom! Boom!"

One after another, the ground shook, gray smoke engulfed the skies, and the overwhelming stench of fumes filled the air. When the smoke cleared, the police escorted me downstairs and out of the front door. In the distance, police escorted my Uncle Max toward me. I broke away from the clutch of the police and ran into my uncle's arms. The police gave us a ride down to the police station. When we arrived at the police station, Mama and the rest of my siblings were waiting on us. The harsh reality had now hit Mama.

My sister and two brothers went with Mama, and I was to join granddad for the summer. When we arrived at granddad's house, he noticed someone inadvertently parked into a parking space that he assumed was his. Ms. Sally and I looked on from inside the car. Granddad hopped out of the car quickly. Despite face-to-face warnings from granddad to move the vehicle from his designated parking spot, his neighbor refused.

"Whoosh!" Granddad forcefully and quickly whipped his hand across the man's face.

"Whoosh!" The man followed suit.

Fury led granddad to hurry away. We rushed behind him. Everywhere he went, I was right there. He went into his apartment. I was there. He went up the stairs, I was there. He pulled out a … wow! Oh no! It was the same L shaped metal structure Marcus had but silver. Granddad scurried to the man's apartment. I scurried behind him. He aimed the L shaped silver metal object at the man and pulled the trigger. The man and granddad were now scuffling on the floor with granddad still holding the metal object.

"Pow! Pow!" Granddad was shooting with no particular aim. The wrestling continued. The man was now in control.

"Pow! Pow!" those sounds again ... This time a bullet had grazed granddad's arm. The same scene emerged again. Police were everywhere. They quickly attended to the man and rushed him in the ambulance. As for my granddad, he left with some circular silver device locked onto his wrists that restrained him. His eyes stayed connected to the ground. This time as the police took him away, we did not follow him. Again, I was mute.

Mama picked me up and took me with her. I did not have any clothes, so we went to a thrift shop. I went to the toy section and mama allowed me to pick anything I wanted. I chose a toy plane into which little men and women could fit and fly away, a General Lee Dukes of Hazzard car from the series and some soldier figures. I had enough with which to play for the rest of the night. Mama went into the bedroom with the door ajar and went to sleep. I too remained mute. The next day Mama thought it would be a distraction to go over to family to celebrate July 4th-Independence Day.

"Crack! Crack! Crack!" The fireworks went off, and so did I back into the house crying uncontrollably. Other family members were popping balloons which added to my agony and I cried and cried and cried even more. *The shootings were happening over and over and over again. Make it stop. Make it stop. I can't move. I can't speak. I can't...*

"Hey y'all," a family member tried to bring a different sound, "Leave him alone! Let him be." I curled up on the bottom of the stairwell leading to the second floor of the house, crying uncontrollably.

Make it stop. Make it stop. I can't move. I can't speak. I can't...

THE FUNERAL

My family was no stranger to loss. In fact, death seemed to have liked our company a bit too much. It had visited my family just about a month prior to hiring Marcus as its assistant. On a street corner in Southeast D.C. and by a woman with a knife as her weapon of choice, Death used her to swipe away the breath of Mama's husband, Mr. Mark Short. I remembered bouncing around on Mom's bed as usual while she was getting dressed. I listened to her as she rationalized her decision regarding Mama's husband's funeral.

"Funerals are no place for kids, boy, even if it is family."

A month later, as I looked onto her lifeless body alone in the coffin, I was taken back a few hours to when we were at my extended family's three-level attached row house home. There were 14 people desperately trying to find a place of solace and Mama and her grandchildren vertically sharing one bed. Even in that cumbersome situation, around the noise and fuss, I felt alone. Even in the discombobulation of taking turns washing ourselves up at the laundry room sink—which had to serve as our washroom for the time being, there was something lifeless in me. One of the older adults in the family, Ms. Jean, attempted to combat my feeling of emptiness right before we were about to leave the house to bid Mom goodbye. We were standing at the door with me on her right side. Ms. Jean grabbed my left shoulder and looked down at me and my eyes met hers. With all her compassion, sincerity, and sheer genuineness, she uttered these words.

"Baby, you're gonna just have to forget about it."

The words resonated so distinctly. How could they not? She was a trusted adult after all and of course she was right. I had to forget about it. I just had to do as she instructed and that was it. That was my mission. So, we walked out the door together and into the limousine.

When we arrived at the funeral home, we exited the limousine together. It was evening but the family was in no hurry. We stood outside for a moment. We did our best to compose ourselves before heading into the church. We crept inside and dragged our feet down the aisle. Finally, we made it to the coffins and stood in front of them. Not too long ago, they had life. Not too long ago, Mama and granddad who were surviving with no help from the government had to scrape all the change they had and also ask family and friends for money to bury their child and grandson. Tony was so still in his coffin. I had not seen him since that dreadful day. I could not forget about it. All that strength I had mustered failed me. My brother was not responding. He just lay there. Unspeakable pain again visited me and brought with it a bucket of tears. I looked again at Mom. Was she never going to get up again? Were we never going to be one with "CP" time heading to school? Were we never again going to be entertained by our own dancing and singing star in our living room? I longed to hear her yelling. I wish she could hear me screaming from within.

"Wake up Mom! Get up! Yell at me. Please!"

My scrawny 10-year-old legs managed to pick themselves up and dashed to Mama sitting in the pews. I sought comfort in her embrace. As that comfort kicked in, it did not take long for me to decide to choose another comfort that awaited me. I scurried outside to the ice cream stand and again acquainted my taste buds with heaven. In and out of the funeral home I went. Moment of hell. Moment of heaven. Once as I was re-entering a moment of hell, I was taken to another tier when I noticed one of the most horrific scenes ever. Tony, who lay lifeless in the coffin, started bleeding from the neck. My little body shook, and I reluctantly found myself yet again at the place and time of that dreadful morning.

He pointed the inverted L shaped black metal structure at Tony's throat and applied pressure to what appeared to be a lever. Tony fell to the ground like a leaf in autumn falling from a tree branch.

In the funeral home, one can imagine how many were gasping and fell to total despair. The wailings were sopranos bouncing off the walls, leaving trails of echo. The men and women in black coats and white gloves tried not to trip over themselves as they scurried up to the altar, wheeled away the casket, attempted to remove all evidence of the red stain, cleaned him up and wheeled the casket back to the altar. This time, if he bled again, the secret would die with him, as the casket was never to be ceremoniously reopened.

"Boy, funerals are no place for kids, even if it is family."

The next day was time for us to take Mom and Tony to where they would be sleeping forever. On the way there, there were all these other limousines and cars driving in one line. I had never seen anything like that before. We arrived at the sleeping place. I also saw another thing that I had never seen before—two big holes about the sizes of Mom's and Tony's caskets. I watched as these men lowered Mom and Tony in those holes—caskets strapped like seat belts. People sang and read Bible scriptures and cried and screamed and threw flowers on the caskets. I never saw a scene like that again. I made sure I did not. One by one, people left; cars drove away. I was one of the last few remaining.

Being forced to say goodbye to the one who gave me life

and to another with whom I shared my life ripped my heart from my body. It is one thing to have felt isolated. It is another to know one fact that not even the police knew—it was I who had opened the door to Death's Assistant. Had I not, would they still have had life? That feeling became my companion.

The FIFTH and SIXTH ELEMENTS

The summer after Mom and Tony's killings seemed to have dragged on forever. No matter how often I hopped over lines and cracks on the sidewalks or in the streets or lines on the supermarket floors or even on the floors in the malls, the lines and cracks never came to an end. They just kept appearing and I kept hopping. The cars were no better either. They too kept appearing. From the hood to the first door, count 1—the first door, count 2—from the first to the second door, count 3—from the second door to the end of the car, count 4. Another car was always right behind. From the hood to the first door, count 1—the first door, count 2—from the first to the second door, count 3—from the second door to the end of the car, count 4. I was in another land far away -- endlessly counting.

"William! Where are you?"

I heard my name from a distance, but I had to put that person on hold, as I did many others. From the hood to the first door, count 1—the first door, count 2—from the first to the second door, count 3—from the second door to the end of the car, count 4. Was this only going to be a summer thing or was time going to lag from now on?

Maybe, it was a normal pace to others, but for me, the pain of losing them trapped me at a stand-still. About five houses up the street was the Smith's house and what I called the neighborhood Day Care. In there, lived the grandmother and grandfather, whose age ranged between 50's and 60's, their four children and three grandchildren—Teresa, about age 8, Trisha, about age 7, Aiden was about age 6, and then there was my friend, Cameron who was about age 8.

As Mama did not like all the neighborhood kids coming to our house, every day after school; other kids and us would become household members of the Smith's house. One thing that stood out to me was that my friend's mom lived in this house with him. Simply put-every second of the day was difficult, but as my elder family member Ms. Jean said, "Baby, you gonna have to forget about it." I did not forget about it. For the first time starting school, Mom was not with me. For the first time in a long time and for that which I could not remember, my siblings and I were on time. For the first time, I longed for the attention that came with being late.

"Bam-Bam, get ready. I am washing you up next."

"Da'Vone, hold still and stop fussing so I could get this wax out your ear ... it's not like I'm using a Q-tip and my nails could scratch you, so hold still."

"Nicci go on over to Mama so she can wash you up while I help wash up your brother."

I listened. I heard only Mama's voice now. Washing up had turned to the same routine as opposed to the excitement of who it was going to be from one morning to the next. We lived in a single parent household with extended family now and had to adapt accordingly.

I still could not forget, as I promised Ms. Jean, but I kept trying. My new neighborhood in Washington DC reminded me that I was not in my old neighborhood of Capitol Heights, where

Mom had died. I hated that there was now a new normal. Walking with the entire block of kids to school just one block away reminded me that there was no school bus to miss leading to "CP" time. There was no walking for miles to get to the second period class. There was, however, in my new school, the feeling of butterflies the first time I stepped into my fifth-grade teacher, Mr. Rockman's classroom. Walking to the third floor was an eternity. Walk up one step, two steps, 10 steps, turn the corner, one more step, five more steps. Why did all of the fifth and sixth graders have to be on the top floor?

Finally, I made it to where the desk and chairs and blackboard were located. I was, however, far from getting comfortable. I tried to pacify myself.

Take deep breaths, William, you can do this. Just open your mouth and let the sounds come out. Stop shaking. Don't say ummm. Just say it.

"Hi. I'm...I'm William."

Now do that many more times. Nobody is going to see you. Nobody knows who you are or our secrets.

"Hi. I'm William."

I did my best to be pleasant while introducing myself to everyone in the class. While I smiled, I was becoming invisible–this way no one could see or hear me. I was not a gift to anyone. I was not a prize to be won. I was not worth having. I was nothing. These feelings engulfed me daily; so did being angry. I was not alive. My heart had stopped beating. I was gasping for air. Am I the only one who was seeing this? I needed to escape.

"Hi. I'm William."

If I could have just withered away that would have been great, but months into fifth grade, I found myself taking on a whole new role -- class comedian. I could hide behind the cloud of laughs and jokes while turning the classroom into a comedy club; especially when I did not know the answers to questions, despite being the know-it-all kid?

"Your comma is in the wrong place. That is not the correct

tense. That is definitely not the way that word is spelt."

Making friends meant learning about each other's mother, father, brother, sister, dog. For me, the topic of my mom and brother was eerie, taboo and was not to be discussed. For my dad, it was easy.

"Where is your dad, William?"

"Oh, he went away to work."

Please don't ask about my mom, please. To everyone in my class, Mom and Tony were still alive because which kid did not have a mom? I avoided talking about them. Deep in the pit of my stomach, I knew the truth, but the shame and embarrassment of not having a mom was something I had to bury. I envied those kids with families. Besides, I was a boy and boys were not allowed to make use of one of the biggest outlets of pain—crying.

As Mr. Know it all, I had an edge over everyone in my class. I decided to become excellent at spelling and grammar and even created my very own spelling bee in my neighborhood. Yes, that's right, I would hold a competition in which contestants were asked to spell a wide selection of words, usually with a varying degree of difficulty, and I, Mr. Know it all would be the judge. Playing school at home was where I felt in control. But, when I was in class, the birds were in control. From outside the windowpane, up, up, up they go. Look out for that cloud!

"Mr. Kellibrew, Mr. Kellibrew."

Wow! Look out for that big piece of cloud coming your way! Dodge!

"Mr. Kellibrew, Mr. Kellibrew!"

As a result, there I was at the blackboard, in front of the entire class, writing multiple times, "I will pay attention in class." My fingers eventually formed a new shape to accommodate holding the chalk and the pencil. Sometimes, it would have been on at least 20 pieces of paper. In fifth grade, I found myself writing a lot for some reason or another. Whether it was due to creating a catapult using my fingers and a rubber band to launch objects at my classmates or making a mockery out of a lesson that refused to connect with me or becoming an act on comic central with the class being the stage, my newly shaped fingers holding the chalk became another painful norm.

I was now the reason kids laughed and it felt good. It was at the expense of others and myself, but my painful days were gone, and an authoritative William had arrived. As I was oftentimes afraid of every turn on a corner because as I did not know what to expect, I built up my do-it-yourself karate moves. I put all that energy I had into becoming Bruce Lee's personal student. Between the Thundercats' character, Cheetara and Bruce Lee, I was quick and very few people could catch me at any given time. Bruce Lee's movies were my Dojo and at times kids were my target practice. I took my practice to the playground at school. Games on the playground which involved fake karate chopping turned out real for me. The other kids also knew it was not practice at all. It was the real deal. That real deal brought with it, aggression, and that aggression brought me problems that had led to my constant recess ban. I often paid the price alone or with some other students that also took it too far.

This extended to home when I kicked the tooth out of my brother's mouth. There went my playtime. I preferred the writing on the board. The fifth grade was not all that bad, especially when I looked across my desk one day and saw Tasha, the girl with whom I had fallen in love at first sight. I had met Tasha during one of my shining introduction moments. We did not talk then but friendship eventually came to us. I really liked Tasha. She was very pretty, and another boy and I used to compete for her attention. She was even so kind to allow us each one day for 60 seconds to be her boyfriend. Once when I was 32 seconds into being her boyfriend, here came the loud, high-pitched sound notifying us that we were to pretend that there was fire in the building. The gaze into her eyes turned into a fire engine rushing water between us. I was so upset and wanted the rest of my 28 seconds. One simply does not forgo 28 seconds of being Tasha's boyfriend.

"Can we keep being girlfriend and boyfriend on the way downstairs?"

Tasha agreed, but the minute was up just as we started to exit the door. I was also mad because Austin, the boy, got his full 60 seconds without being interrupted. One also does not share a girl like Tasha, so I challenged the other boy to a fight in the third-floor bathroom.

"Mr. Rockman, can I have a pass to the bathroom?"

Not long after, I found out that Austin also got a pass as he opened the door and turned the corner into the bathroom. I stood there and looked up to his tall stature and pushed his shoulder. His friendship with me would not allow him to lift his hands to strike back. He must have thought I really was a clown because he left me standing there.

Mr. Rockman thought that I needed some discipline and something to take my time up, so he asked Mr. Mason, the gym teacher, to allow me to be a safety patrol, which was making sure that everyone who was crossing the street did so safely. No one was going to get hit on my watch. Kids had to have great grades and be honorable amongst their peers to be a safety patrol. They made an exception for me. I was super excited, and I took my job of saving lives very seriously. I was even promoted to Captain of the Safety Patrols at my school. I felt like I was needed. I even participated in the Safety Patrol Parade in Washington D.C. Safety patrols would come from across America. We would march in front of the White House where the President of the United States lived–from one end to the other. All those days and long hours of practicing were not in vain.

"Left, left, left, right, left."

The President was watching us! Wow!

"Left, left, left, right, left."

One person who took me seriously was Ms. Cox, my creative writing teacher. She was also the spelling bee teacher. If one wanted to be in the spelling bee they would have to go through Ms. Cox. Practicing for the spelling bee meant that we had to become good writers and show our use of vocabulary words by writing essays. My first essay with Ms. Cox shocked her. I had written an essay titled, "I Didn't Know Blood Could Fly." The depiction of Mom's blood being splattered everywhere as she was being killed caught Ms. Cox's attention, who then brought it to my sixth-grade teacher, Ms. Kathy, unbeknownst to me. Ms. Kathy decided to put me to full use by making me the Friday afternoon substitute teacher during spelling test time.

The end of the summer was here, and sixth grade had arrived. I was super thrilled to be sitting next to my 60 second girlfriend, Tasha. We would talk so much that our teacher would move me to a different seat. She started to recognize the spelling bee master in me and like Mr. Rockman, assigned me to help others and even made me the librarian of the class. My powers even included correcting students' papers. My powers stopped working when it came to my paying attention in class.

So, while the class was learning new things, I was busy excelling at being the librarian. Organizing books was my job. I could not wait to get home because I would create school at home. One day in school away from home, we all had to choose a country to research. For some reason, West Germany was mine. America had chosen to support her while Russia had taken the other country on the other side of the Berlin Wall–East Germany.

The teacher put us in pairs to work on this project and my other half, the cool walking Tyrone nicknamed Lo Lo, hailed from Missouri in his tennis shoes, plaid shirts untucked, and a hair pick in his head. I was not happy. This was my solo project, and this guy was not to be a part of it. Forced into partnership, I discovered that I was not alone in my pain. Tyrone had lost his mom in a car accident. Just like that, Tyrone and I were now friends. Not only were we partners on the West Germany project, but he lived just a few blocks from me, and we became close. I was a chatterbox and so was Tyrone.

When the report cards came out, Ms. Kathy handed me my fate in my hands. I walked the one block home that translated into miles holding the sealed envelope. I handed it to Mama, and she opened it. Sitting beside her, I did not know what to anticipate. Mama read the report from top to bottom, but when she got to the bottom, we both noticed in the comment section in Ms. Kathy's teacher handwriting, "William is too loquacious."

"I don't know what that means," said Mama "but you betta get it together." I was eager to know what that big word meant so as usual, I turned to my friend, the dictionary. There it was, right beside loquacious, was talkative. I kept being loquacious all the way to prom season.

I decided to ask my 60 second girlfriend but she had other plans. She chose a new guy, Howie. He was big enough to intimidate me if he wanted to do so. He actually liked my sister so that gave me the courage I needed. I was very protective of my sister Nicci, and nobody was going to date her without going through me, and that was that. So, Howie went to the prom with Tasha, and I went to the prom with the girl that had no date. Carrie and I were happy going together. As prom signifies the celebration of the end, I had to say goodbye to sixth grade.

Choosing Shaw Junior High School where all the classrooms had no walls was not compatible with my desire to be a nuisance to one set of kids and a teacher. Soon thereafter, I would ride my first bus, well buses in this case, to a new school called Langley. For now, though, duty would call for me at the Playmakers.

THE SPIRIT OF IRA ALDRIDGE

They said that Mom and Tony were now asleep forever. Maybe one day they would become awakened. There was not much sleep where I lay my head. Still, I wished Mom and Tony were here in the chaos with me. With life after Mom, 14 people now slept under the same roof at our new address—biological relatives and as a result of the Good Samaritan Act. There were cots everywhere. There were cots in the living room. There were cots in the dining room. There were cots in the basement. This was not like the basement with the ice cream parlor. There was no sneaking around here.

No fewer than three people slept on Mama's bed. We would rotate on different nights. There was a loud crowd for breakfast. There was a loud crowd for lunch during summers. There was a loud crowd for dinner. There was a loudness for which I longed at the dinner table, so maybe if I waited long enough, Mom and Tony would join us and make more noise. Mom's loudness was not the only thing I missed. I missed my Matchbox cars and Hot Wheels collection. As an avid child car collector, having to leave all my cars back at our old house was devastating, so I started over.

Mama could not resurrect my mom nor Tony nor could she replace the bond and memories I had developed with my car collection, but she vowed, silently, to do her best to help replace that which she could. She took us to thrift stores and voila! There were cars! Though I was happy, it was different because the feeling was never the same starting a new relationship as opposed to enjoying one already established. Nonetheless, this was going to have to do. I started building new cities, new roads, invented new addresses, for my new cars and I to go. Building a new world was not easy but it was necessary.

The summer after Mom and Tony's death brought with it, new life. The life about five doors down from us involved new faces with which to make friends and I did, with Cameron. I did not know the blessings that were to come from my new best friend, Cameron and all those new smiling faces of children everywhere. It was different and uncomfortable being the new kid on the block. My car collection, however, made me the engineer on the block.

My mom's DNA catapulted me to a social interaction guru and solidified my role as the entertainer of the century as far as 10-year olds living a block away from Howard University's campus in Washington, D.C, were concerned. I danced well; I sang well; and I was the lead singer in our pretend New Edition groups. Of course, I was Ralph Tresvant and "Mr. Telephone Man" and "Cool it Now" echoed Bryant Street. Who knew that all the years my mom made me get up in front of the family and sing and perform was her manager's moment of preparing me for my artist moment. One of the days, during my Ralph Tresvant transformation, when I was doing a superb job hiding the hollowness within me, and still managed to put on quite a show, my performance caught the attention of Melvin Andrews, who was walking down the street minding his own business. He asked me where I lived and if I would mind taking him to meet my parents. He did not meet my parents, but he did meet Mama. He was saying something about a group he was a part of, or

something to that effect, and though he had Mama's attention,
I scurried back to being Ralph Tresvant.

When I returned home, Mama became Melvin's mouthpiece
and picked up from where I had run off back to my ever so important
performance. In all that Mama was saying, I learned that I would be
auditioning for a group called the Kelsey E. Collie Playmakers
Repertory Company founded by Howard University Professor
Kelsey E. Collie.

When I auditioned at Howard, I was to recite a monologue
and sing a song. I did not know what that big word meant but I did
know a song. So, there I was in Ira Aldridge Theatre ready to sing
Whitney Houston's Greatest Love of All. But why were there only
two or three people in that huge auditorium? They were in the center
and next to each other. Ralph Tresvant was now terrified. I did
notice the man I brought to my grandmother and felt a little, just a
little more at ease.

The time came for me to recite the monologue and shortly
after I began, I heard, "okay, okay, thank you." Why were they
thanking me? Was it over? That's it? All my years of unknowingly
preparing had brought me to this? Perhaps those three people in
that huge theater, with seats lining the backs of those chairs, did not
mean to say those words. So I got ready and delivered my acapella.

"I believe the children are our future, treat them well and let
them lead the way. Show them all the beauty they possess inside..."

"Okay, okay, thank you."

What?! "Okay, okay, thank you," was all they said after I sang my
heart out. They did it again. That was not a fluke. What was happening? Why did he ask me to audition if they were not going to
listen to me? Not too long after, for another contestant, there was
another "okay, okay, thank you." I guess that was what they did. I
looked around in the Green Room where all of us contestants were
waiting to hear from the "okay, okay, thank you people " about who
was chosen. Some of us were pacing back and forth. I noticed they

had their parents with them. Mama was home because we had no babysitter. I had already bitten my nails down when Melvin came inside the room. Maybe their "okay, okay, thank you" was them thanking me in advance for choosing to accept their invitation to join the group. They actually chose me to join the Playmakers. My mom manager's role with me as her star entertainer had paid off on stage. She was still sleeping. I did not know what was to become of me off stage. My nerves were still tingling all over my body as this was the start of a new pathway.

SEVENTH GRADE

Langley Junior High School featured it's three squares-like floors with their classrooms wrapped around a hollow of nothingness right down the middle gave spark to my already budding imaginary world that came more alive every day. Who would we be chasing in circles around these hallways? Wow! The view from the third floor all the way down was nothing short of spectacular! Langley was a huge school. It was my mission to learn of every nook and cranny in this building.

Once, a couple of friends and I decided to explore the underground area of the school. We found a tunnel through an opening in the basement near the gym and started to climb through the tunnels hearing that there had been a link between Langley and McKinley Tech High School underground. We crawled through "crawl spaces" and through still water to get to the other side. Exposed pipes above our heads caused barriers for standing and small corridors prevented us from walking through. We crawled our way through and wiggled our way through until finally we found an opening that indeed was across the parking lot to the high school. "Wow! A parade!" The McKinley Tech parade was one of the biggest events in our neighborhood and city. We blended into the parade with Langley in the backdrop.

These were my first days of learning how to play hooky from class. It took me back to the crawl spaces of that big white house on the hill where my siblings and I played hide and seek. I was going to love this school. I loved even more my homeroom teacher who happened to be my first period teacher. She was French. Who needed Tasha when you had a French teacher?

As different as the language was to me, so were the folks I met in my homeroom. That did not matter though. I was the unconquerable William who dominated the spelling bee. I was the unconquerable William who was the teacher's aide. I was the unconquerable William who was now a part of the Playmakers. I was the unconquerable William who represented my school on the track team in elementary school and dominated whenever I played games in my neighborhood. I was now taking the bus on my own. Gone were the days when I had to sneak off the block and hurry back to ensure Mama's eyes landed on me when she was doing her rounds of checking. Now, I walked regularly off the block with my new friends Andy, Samuel and Gregory. Despite the company, I was alone. Nonetheless, we would not stop walking until we arrived in our homeroom. This new terrain called middle school demanded a new level of trust between Mama and me. Unconquerable as I was, there was something that conquered me.

At all times, as much as possible, I had to remain covered. Having a coat on even in the heated classrooms made me feel safe, warm and comforted. I wondered if this kid Derrick in my homeroom felt comforted knowing he was wearing the cleanest tennis shoes in the entire school along with the latest name brand. There was however one moment when I could feel similar to how he was feeling. I was at my locker and despite many attempts of inputting my code, it would not open. With my confusion came a sudden heavy thump pain from behind to my stomach and rib cage. I was instantaneously on all four crunched over.

"Why you goin in my locker n*#@*!"

I could not catch my breath. I looked up and saw Derrick, the biggest and tallest dude in seventh grade, staring down at me. I managed to get a few words out.

"It's my locker. Number 301."

"That's not this locker n*#@*, it's that one."

When I looked at the lockers, I realized the locker I had was actually a different number. I had made a mistake. Derrick went on to open his locker and I went to crawl my way from the floor. As time went on, Derrick and I were at our lockers at class changes because of the new normal called middle school; so was his notice of me in our homeroom. He also took notice that I was excellent at speaking French and writing French. That brought us to the negotiation table. I would become his tutor and in return, he would be my protector in school instead of my bully.

"If you have any problems with anyone, let me know and I'll take care of it," Derrick firmly uttered. That worked for me. He was one of the nicest dudes, when his fist was not saying hello to parts of my body. I got to know Derrick well. I also learned things few people knew. In his locker, were hundreds and thousands of dollars safely tucked away. From time to time, I would see him carry this wad of money away. I found out that his uncle was Ray, one of the biggest drug dealers in D.C. at the time and that Derrick was one of his soldiers. I stuck to my French with Derrick, and he stuck to protecting me. I never used his services, but Derrick took a liking to me and out of a lot of fear, I made sure I did not cross him and that he passed his French class.

Like French, I was really doing well in most of my other classes. Not only was I keeping up with my classes, I continued to be stellar at being the class clown. That stellar behavior caught the attention of the assistant principal whose job was to discipline those who were great at being disruptive. Like any great negotiator, Mama

made me an offer I could not refuse. If at the end of the year, I
retired from the clown act, I would join the Playmakers to perform
in Ireland. That deal required all my teachers and the principal
to report the same positive news. Lucky for me, that deal did not
involve passing all my classes.

    "Everyone must change their clothes into gym attire or sit
out and fail the course," my teacher said.

    I was not taking off my coat. I was not taking off my clothes
in the boys' locker room. They were not going to strip my comfort
and safety from me. Week 1, I sat on the sidelines and watched the
kids play volleyball, one of the sports I loved to play. Week two,
I sat on the sidelines and watched the kids play basketball. Week
40, I sat on the sidelines and watched the kids play flag football. I
picked up all my passing grades from my other classes and the F
from gym and packed my bags for Ireland.

THE PLAYMAKERS

The history of my ancestors as well as legends, such as Rosa Parks, Daniel Hale Williams, Dr. Martin Luther King Jr., and others within the African American community were introduced to me through the art of the Playmakers in a deeper fashion. Self-awareness, pride and understanding the journey that has brought my ancestors to this hour were possible through the work of the Playmakers. Through plays, we saw black images and experienced black reflections. Melvin and Mr. Collie were our everyday images.

Melvin was like a dad to Tony Martin and I. Tony was like a little brother. I grew close with the Playmakers. I used acting and performing to hide in plain sight. I embraced it. I loved it. I was good at it. I was even good at dancing. My family was so excited when they came to my first performance in Ira Aldridge Theater. It was huge. I knew all things were possible then if little me was performing on such a big stage. I really came to appreciate how theater became a medium for me, taking me far away from that dreadful morning in Capitol Heights. I was able not to be William Kellibrew, the traumatized kid.

One thing that I remembered well in theater was substitution.

To become in character, I had to think of something or a moment in the past in which that situation resonated with what I was trying to portray. One day I was playing a character who was given harsh news and I cried on the spot. Well, that was easy. Navigating my emotions was a release for me. I relished it. I became popular. You could have found me on Black Entertainment Television's Teen Summit-a popular TV show, and even on news stations talking about the Playmakers. Yep, this new William was outspoken, articulate and was high in demand. Not only was I high in demand but the Playmakers were so awesome, they made sure we were high in the sky.

We traveled to the Bahamas and performed. We traveled to Toronto, Canada and performed in the Caribana, one of the largest celebrations of Caribbean people outside of the Caribbean. We even traveled to Dundalk, Ireland to perform in the Maytime Festival including in the town square. Again, I was one of the ones chosen to give an interview. Thanks to Mama's $87 and the fund raising from the Playmakers, I lived. It was hard though leaving my family and knowing that siblings were not able to join me. It was not hard though, flying from Washington, D.C. to JFK International Airport in New York City and taking a TWA airplane and transferring to Aer Lingus to Ireland. Nope, it was not hard as I had brought some friends with me—my Matchbox and Hot Wheels cars. Forgetting them on the shuttle bus at JFK caused difficulty in breathing for everyone as I created quite a panic alarm and the only way for us to return to steady breathing was to have the shuttle bus return and deliver my toy cars to me.

My cars and I watched in awe at the majestic ocean below. We took in the picturesque view driving up to Dundalk from Dublin and then arriving at the Imperial Hotel. We noticed that they had a completely different accent from the British accent. Perhaps it was because they were Irish and had an Irish accent.

Seeing Black people in Ireland then, was like seeing a giraffe strolling in Times Square, New York City. It simply did not happen, I heard from the locals. There was much fuss in seeing the Black people who had arrived, and more amazingly, we did not dribble and shoot ball for a living.

Still, we were celebrities and they treated us as such-kind, warm and in awe of us. There was one basketball player we did not know, staying at the same Imperial Hotel, who received a lot of attention with his towering figure and caramel skin. As usual, we performed at their festival in our celebrity fashion. Perhaps, I was too carefree. I had lost my passport and thankfully Melvin found it. I had joined Marlon and Daryl and climbed a mountain, singing at the top of our voices, the Black National Anthem, "Lift Every Voice and Sing." It started to rain. We heard that other Playmakers did this in the past.

I decided to trot down the mountain. Trotting turned into running. I was running uncontrollably and then flipped in the air; hit a rock, flipped in the air again, landed on my back, which knocked the wind out of me. My camera and whatever else were in my hand flew away and I spent several minutes in the mud and rain trying to find what was gone from me. I made it to the base of the mountain on our bus and was told to change by Melvin, my saving grace. My mind raced quickly as to how I could shy away from everyone and change my clothes so no one could see me; so I went outside to the back of the bus. My eyes kept watching the corner of the bus for someone to interrupt me hiding. My nerves were on high alert. That was soon overshadowed by the memories of going to the malls or walking down the streets.

Back home in America, many stayed with the group in Play-makers and went on to amazing careers; a star of Family Matters – Kellie Shanygne Williams, others gracing the stage on Broadway – Daryl Spiers, nationally known comedians and singers, and even coaching on the American Idol and the Oscars—Nick Cooper.

For me, things had turned the other way. Boys wearing

leotards as I did in dancing with the Playmakers caused others to bully and make fun of me. Outside of the Playmakers, people would tease me and call me gay in an attempt to hurt me, as such was seen as a negative label. I was 10 years old. Defenseless. What did I know? I knew I was now going to skip as many dance classes as I could and I did. I knew I was going to be very self-conscious of my body and I was. I knew being called gay, a punk was stirring up a dark place inside and it did. I knew that dark place would one day escape from the inside and sit boldly on the outside. It further chomped at my dignity and self-esteem.

THE BRIDGE

The return from Ireland landed me close to the end of the seventh grade. Perhaps it was because the deal was over, but I returned to the days of mischief. With that came more than one failing class. Summer also came and went. Eighth grade came and I was not with my usual peers. The students were different. Many could not read or write. The work looked all too familiar; wait, I had done this work before.

"Excuse me, but I think I am in the wrong class. I am supposed to be in the eighth grade."

"This is the eighth grade. Special education."

I did not know what to do. I was confused with very little to no information to help me solve this riddle. They did not say I learn differently. Was I being punished? I felt the humiliation in my stomach even being seen going into the special education classroom. I kept my head down in the class and when questions were asked about some assignment, I would be quick to answer the question correctly to show my knowledge and to show that these classes were not for me. I had to distract myself. I started to explore around the school. My music teacher, Ms. Pamela Alexander would allow me to enter her class. I did sometimes. I would find myself staring outside the window for lengths at a time.

"William, do you want to join the chorus line?"

Marcus pointed the inverted L shape black metal structure at Tony's throat, and applied pressure to what appeared to be a lever.

Tony fell to the ground like a leaf in autumn falling from a tree branch.

"William?"

The chorus line seemed like a great idea. Performing was my thing after all and so I did with West Side Story. For the first time, I sang in the auditorium in front of all my peers. This was not Ireland. There was no standing ovation. This was a room full of teenagers in a public school in an underserved neighborhood in Washington D.C. It was awkward. It was uncomfortable.

Nonetheless, I continued to perform. I sang. I danced. The more I performed, the more my anxiety grew. Were they looking at me? What were they seeing? Where can I hide? Even in my neighborhood, I could not hide. Folks in the neighborhood would call me crazy and label me because of my hyper behavior. They knew something was very different about me. I really just needed to be gone. This desire to disappear was happening more and more.

One day I woke up with an eerie feeling in my stomach that such a day was not going to be good. I told myself, today was the day I wanted it all to end. I rose from the bed. I hid the bedding from where I had wet it with my pee. That seemed to be an every night affair. I got dressed. I put on my smelly socks and shoes as it had been days since they were cleaned. I grabbed my school bag and my bag of despair and strapped them on my back. I grabbed the $5 Mama had left for me to purchase lunch and two bus tokens. The bus was not going to be necessary that morning. I walked up to North Capitol Street, N.E. and Rhode Island Avenue.

As I walked on the bridge, I stopped. I slowly turned to face the incoming traffic below me. I leaned my body against the brace.

I leaned it over some and some more. In a few moments, the never-ending nightmare would be over? I opened the door to the man that would take Mom and Tony from me forever. I opened the door. I am here. They are not. A plunge would be quick. Headfirst. I could now be with Mom and Tony.

Wait. Would I go to heaven or hell? Would I see Mom and Tony again? Would I dishonor my family?" Tears and confusion slapped me around.

I slowly pulled up. I would try again at 3 p.m. when I got out of school. I continued walking till I found myself in my home-room period. Though the class was packed, I heard no one. I saw no one. All I saw was death. I had met the gates of hell. I was unworthy to be alive. The invisible thing that was weighing on me was so heavy, it was pounding me into the ground, but was it not mine to carry? After homeroom, I decided that I could not go to another class. I had to go to a sanctuary in the school, Mr. Christian's office.

"William," he told me once, "if you cannot sit in class then the first place you need to come is my office, and we will discuss what is happening."

I do not know if I could have discussed what I did not know but I know I needed an escape, and fast. As I sat in his office, Mr. Christian noticed that I was not my usual self and that I looked like the world had ended. He must have seen death on me as I was wreaking it. Next thing I knew, my grandmother contacted Children's Hospital National Medical Center and arranged for my first ever assessment. Strangely, they allowed me to walk myself to the hospital. But, of course to them it was not strange, they did not know what I knew. Again, I arrived at that bridge. Hope. I held on tightly, squeezed onto it really hard, and hurried across. I made it. I made it to the other side.

Later that day, I was somehow admitted into an adult program at George Washington University Hospital. Apparently, I had missed the Children's Hospital by one year. I was now 13. I was admitted into the George Washington University Psychiatry Unit – 6-North. This was the strangest place I had ever been. I was told that I could not come out of my bedroom unless I had to use the bathroom and even then, I had to be watched. They said I was on suicide watch, and I remembered being in my gown, isolated in my room trying to figure out where I would go from here. The nurses kept coming in and taking my blood samples. I would pull back and resist.

"No! No! Not again. Not more blood!"

As I fought, and was near fainting, the nurses would calm me and bring me water. They were puzzled as to my reaction to blood. I was not puzzled. With every drop of blood they took, I felt the deepening loss of my soul and spirit. Finally, I was out and had to be revived.

PART I

Reflections

Looking back at the moment on the bridge, I had reached an inflection point. I felt broken beyond repair. Trying to forget my mother, my brother, and what happened to me proved impossible. The weight of it was too heavy and I questioned why I should continue existing.

All of the atrocities flooded my thoughts, my emotions, and my physical body. I was hanging on by a string. I thought about my grandmother, Mama. I thought about my family. I was afraid of the unknown if I let go.

One thing kept me clinging to the bridge and my book-bag. That one thing was a bright idea of hope. I was afraid to live and I was afraid to die but I imagined that if I could hold on for a few more moments someone would save me, someone would take the weight off of my body – and he did.

PART II

Turning Point

William keynoted the DYCD and the Mental Health Association of NYC's Healing the Hurt Conference at New York Law School. His talk focused on Values and Healing as a lead trainer for the Substance Abuse and Mental Health Services Administration's National Center for Trauma Informed Care, a project of the National Association of State Mental Health Program Directors, 2017,

Photo: JuRon McMillan.

MS. PIERRE

We were allowed visitors from time to time, but only key family members such as my grandmother. Seeing the adults and some older teens in this space was eye-opening. I witnessed staff having challenges with patients and patients struggling to find themselves. It made me reflect upon my life and what my future would look like. After thirty days, a professional made the determination that I was not a threat to myself or others and so I was released from George Washington University Psychiatry Unit – 6-North. I was now cleared to resume my life. What life? My release from the psychiatric unit was my checking into outpatient therapy at the children's hospital. No one ever did explain to me how I was an adult in the psychiatry unit but a child in outpatient.

Anything we talked about is confidential except … the famous rule of therapy. You can say anything to me, and it will be confidential except if you tell me that you want to hurt yourself … except if you tell me you want to hurt others. That made sense. It also made sense to me to have kept my wanting to jump off the bridge to myself—and I did.

On the first day of outpatient, Mama accompanied me as we sat in the lobby. A slender dark-skinned woman, with a non-American yet peculiar accent, that did not remind of Ireland but more of the characters on television that were from England, introduced herself as Ms. Christine Pierre. With her stark difference from anything I have known, she had me at hello. With that hello came goodbye from Mama's presence. Ms. Pierre must have used one of those intuitive therapist powers because she paused our session and took me to the cafeteria. How did she know? Anything would have been appetizing! Ms. Pierre asked one question that partially released me from one of the prisons in which I was trapped.

"What do you want for lunch?" She asked.

What did I want? Wow! Was this woman for real? What did I want? I wanted many things. I wanted my family not to be displaced. I wanted to have my own room again. I did not want to be living with family members outside of Mama, Rodney, Nicci, Da'Vone, and Cody. Wait. She did not ask me what I wanted. She asked me what I wanted to eat. Well in that case, that ice cream machine and I were on the verge of becoming best friends. This time, there was no 007 crawling in and out of windows into basements. This was in the open with no alert sensors on duty. I bonded with the ice cream machine, and weeks with her turned into months.

"Did you enjoy your ice-cream, William? Ms. Pierre began the session again.

"Yep," my swinging legs and elevated cheeks must have made that clear.

"Is home as much fun as ice-cream?"

My swinging legs came to a halt, my body slouched, my face dropped, and my eyes met the floor.

"Home is not fun most of the time."

"How is it not fun most of the time William?"

"Well for one thing, Mama yells at us all the time. Her voice is screeching, and it feels like it is cutting through our ears. I don't like when Mama yells.

"You ever tried laughing when your mama yells?"

Laugh? That was a weird question. What does that have to do with anything?

One day Nicci, Brian and I were in the back of the car going somewhere with Mama. Her voice suddenly went into the usual opera mode except the sound coming from her was not appealing. My ears hurt as usual.

"You ever tried laughing when your mama yells?" I heard Ms. Pierre clearly.

I then, as quietly as I could, made short, repeated spurts of silly gasps. They were so infectious, my siblings followed.

"What y'all sniggling about?!" Mama's voice snapped from the front seat.

We would simmer down until the next opportunity to laugh. While this was feeling good, I could only laugh about 10 percent of the time. The other 90% was crushing my soul. I could not wait to get back to the one place where I felt as good as I was going to feel.

"So, William, can you describe how Mama's yelling makes you feel?" Ms. Pierre's curious mind continued.

"I feel very bad because I think she is mad, and it makes me feel worse. I don't like that I make her mad."

"Feels worse?"

"Yes. Worse than how I already feel."

"Would you mind telling me what you are feeling bad about?"

Tears flooded my eyes. Tears burned my eyes. Tears started to trickle.

"It's my fault. I let him in. Then he killed them and let me go. It's my fault and I don't want to make Mama more mad." Ms. Pierre's eyes were piercing. It was as if she was trying to reach through my soul. Someone sees me. Someone is listening to me. Not just anyone, but someone who makes me feel different than anyone else...makes me feel as if what I say, or feel is important. But

I was only 13, so how did my voice matter?

"He killed my mom and Tony."

For the first time, I felt a release. For the first time, I told someone my secret ... what I made happen and how I can never bring back Mama, her daughter or her grandson.

I loved these sessions with Ms. Pierre. They were making me feel better. I still wanted my mom and Tony to come back, but I was slowly grasping the idea ... maybe Ms. Pierre was right, I did not make him do it. I could not wait for the next session.

As the sessions continued, I started to feel more relaxed. Finally, someone I could trust. Since the dreadful morning of July 2nd, 1984, I was able to exhale. I was slowly beginning to breathe again. This was my moment to fight. This was my moment to slowly see my way out of that room from that dark morning and find my way to life. Hope was seeping its way to me."

"William, these times with you were so amazing for me and I cannot thank you enough for sharing your thoughts and your feelings with me. I want to let you know that I will not be your therapist. We have a few more sessions and we have to start transitioning to another therapist."

There it went. Hope for a lifetime with Ms. Pierre. I was intrigued at the next chapter, but very sad about Ms. Pierre leaving.

Ms. Pierre introduced me to the new person. After a while it didn't work, and I was off to finding a new person who would listen to me and give me some ice cream.

"Take out the trash! Pick up your clothes! Stop all that playing!" The opera voice was even more poignant.

This was no laughing matter.

The one thing I had going for me with which I was very comfortable—making someone laugh as the class clown.

SECOND ROUND

The no laughing matter trend seeped its way throughout many episodes in my life. One of those especially pertained to one of my family members echoing the words, "I'll beat you outta of a merry dream." Her words manifested when she used the vicious sting of a belt to awaken me. It was the worst feeling. I was caught in a trap. I was beaten for wetting the bed or being disobedient in school. I was paralyzed in fear of walking in the dark to use the bathroom so I would not wet the bed. That fear projected an alternative reality where I was made to believe that the bed was the bathroom. I knew that was an illusion when I started to feel the wetness come across the bed.

"Darn!"

There it was again. Laying in my urine all night was more comforting than getting up in the dark and moving around the house. It was also the shame that persisted so much that I was afraid that my family would recognize that I did indeed wet the bed again. No one wanted to sleep with me. I was often relegated to my own sleeping bed and by the time one month or year passed, the stains were literally unbearable. It worsened. As it was the birthright of the older siblings to bully the younger, I showed no mercy to my younger brother and sister. My older siblings and family members showed none to me. My feet turned outward instead of inward when I walked. To my siblings and family members, that was a gay thing. Hence, the mockery and ridicule jumped all over me. Walk away, my older siblings and cousins would command me. I could see their faces from the back of my head as tears formulated on the front. Their eyes popped over, head kicked back, jaws spread and teeth glowing as sounds of joy busted upward from within them. That sound was so taunting and so devastating that I made a daily appointment with my feet to change the direction of my walk. Turn inward not outward. Do it again....and again...and again. That's it... you got it William.

One day, I was standing in the foyer with my brothers, sister and cousins, and they again brought their ridicule. They started to tease me and bully me again. I had made up my mind that I was through with these bullies. I did what was not allowed in our family.

"Shit!"

I could not believe I just cursed at them. They told Ms. Jean that I had cursed, and she stormed down the hallway, and towered over me.

"What did you say?!" she screamed.

For the second time in my life, I was faced with my biggest bully and for the second time, I had to stand up for myself. I was through with these bullies.

"I said shit!"
She cocked her heavy-handed hand back to the right as far

as she could and twisted her body. She must have put every ounce of her weight into that swing, and she let it rip with me standing there waiting for that smackdown. It landed directly on the left side of my face, turning my head around like the exorcist, except my head could only go so far. I was determined to introduce her to the moment Harpo hit Sofia–Oprah Winfrey's character–in the 1985 movie, "The Color Purple." With my head still turned around to the right, my eyes closed, my fist balled up, I mustered every piece of strength I had and landed a fist in her face and she fell back. Everyone was hysterical and could not believe this had happened. I felt like they provoked it, but I was not going to let someone do that to me one more time. I had had enough slaps in my face and the only person I would ever accept that from was my mother when she slapped me in the face when I turned into a snarky 9-year-old—like I had a choice anyway.

"Mom, Mom, Mom!" It was mom, for everything.

"Don't you know any other name other than mom!!!???"

"Jackie?"

I saw my body being hoisted across the room from the slap across my face from Mom that lifted me. I never forgot that feeling and I never forgot what landed me there.

As Ms. Jean and I tussled and fought, everyone was hyped around us. She pounced on me. Wham! Another slap. Eventually, she got me on the outside of the house and down the porch stairs. My decision to fight back, perhaps it was fighting an adult, changed the trajectory of a four-year relationship I deemed as a prison of fear.

"Don't you ever come back to my house boy!" She was cursing at me and demeaning me.

"F*#@ you B*#@!"

71

An older cousin pinned me down to the ground trying to keep me calm. Surprisingly, Ms. Jean came over to me and beat me in my face with an oversized plastic bat. I was completely unprotected and trapped. I could not do anything. I could not run. I could not block myself and I just had to take the pain and beating that she thought I had deserved. When she stopped beating me and he let me up, I went to my neighbor's house where I called my godfather. That night, they took me to the hospital, and I was hospitalized for the second time in my life. For some strange reason, I felt like I was not the only one that needed to be hospitalized. For gone were the nights I had shared with Ms. Jean and the good times shrouded by the fearful times; the times we used to stay up all night playing games and the times we shared meals and laughs.

Here I was again at George Washington University Hospital. This time, there was no Ms. Pierre. There was more blood, more invasion of my personal space, but a chance to take a breath and be with some patients who may have understood what I was going through. Something must have landed them in this terrible place. Maybe they were not so different from me. I was done with life. I was done with everything. Unfortunately, it was a family member. It cost me everything; my living arrangement, and my family being separated for the second time. Again, I had been displaced from my family. Again, I was not allowed on the premises to retain my property. Mama had to collect all my belongings. Life as I knew it again came to a sudden halt.

In the first hospitalization, I attended a workshop called AA, but had no clue what that meant. I just remember sitting in a circle and everyone introducing themselves.

"Hello, my name is Michael, and I am an alcoholic."
When it was my turn, it was "Hi, I am William, a patient."

Everyone remarked, "Hello William."

By the end of that experience, we all quoted this saying together that hung as a banner across the wall – "God grant me the serenity to accept the things that I cannot change, courage to change the things that I can, and the wisdom to know the difference." I never forgot that saying and I attempted to comprehend it. It was of use. I remained confused. However, on the day when I fought Ms. Jean, I felt there was something brewing inside of me that I could change. Ms. Jean was old-school traditional and did not put up with kids talking back or not following instructions from adults. Ms. Jean was great when she was great, but harsh when she was harsh. As a teenager, it was hard to accept physical aggression from anyone other than Mom. Change brewed. I was going to change who would receive the opportunity to beat upon me. For some, it may have looked like I was completely out of control. For me, I wondered how many of them that stood on that street and living in that house, needed to be right there with me on my second visit to George Washington University Hospital Psychiatric Unit.

When I got out of the hospital, Mama reminded me that I would not be going back to my family member's house and Mama did not want to ruffle feathers. I expected that. I was in the ninth grade trying to finish out the year as strong as I could, in hopes of graduating. I had chosen to attend Duke Ellington School of the Arts and start on my journey as a vocalist. My godfather offered me an opportunity to stay with him and his mom, whom I affectionately called grandma. I had to quickly learn a lot more about being an adult than I had expected. I faithfully took the bus from the Southeast and traveled from one end of the city to the other simply to attend Duke Ellington School of the Arts.

"You ever tried laughing William?" There went Ms. Pierre again.

This was no laughing matter.

" *God grant me the serenity to accept the things that I cannot change, courage to change the things that I can, and the wisdom to know the difference.* "

— Serenity Prayer

FAMILY THERAPY

I knew the social worker intern known as Ms. Pierre was gone. I knew I did not like any other therapists. I knew I had to remain in therapy. I knew that even more so when I met the full-time social worker who was to carry on the baton.

The race to healing was certainly going to be a marathon with several team players. Like Ms. Pierre, the full-time social worker, was distinct from me culturally. She appeared to be from the Mediterranean, and I could not tell, but unlike the intern, she was steady in her tone, direct in her questioning and carried an almost stern-like energy. Her approach was as if she had declared war on my fears, my anxieties, my inhibitions and whether or not I was on board; she was Team William even if that meant going up against me. She brought my mind to corners of my being to which I was unaware existed. Those thought-provoking sessions shook me to my core. Through her approach, I joined her on Team William. Apparently so did Mama, as this full-time social worker, the commander would have her join our sessions.

They also continued preparation for the race of life without me being on the track. Before I knew it, other players joined the team—my siblings, and my father, but this time with new coaches. This time, the therapy sessions which would be later used for trainings by the therapists, were being filmed at Walter Reed Hospital Army Medical Center. I was 15 or 16 when the family sessions began.

Within these training grounds, we started to identify impediments that were keeping us from fully performing—the murder of Mom and Tony were ever present within our spirit. My sister was sexually abused, Mama was sexually abused; Mom was bisexual, maybe my life did not exist. This team was intricately woven by a common thread-trauma. The camera persons were glued to this race and instead of cheering for a favorite team or athlete, there were tears of overwhelming sorrow. They continued throughout the first year, second year, third year, thirteenth year.

One day after the 13th year, I crossed paths with one of the camera persons. She was quite elated as if I had risen from the dead. I must have risen to her as she expressed pure joy in seeing that I was alive and well. How could it be, she inquired. Those tears of sorrow I now learned was her way of cheering for the team. She cheered for the evidence that hope and light will always, if one allows them, battle darkness and win. She brought me back to one of the impediments that showed itself during our family sessions. Mine.

PIERCING of the SOUL

Mom was friendly with a lot of people. Our house was open to just about anyone. Everywhere we lived, King Square, Dodge View. If it was up to her, we would have taken in the world. She was kind-hearted and congenial, and sometimes to our detriment.

All the kids in our neighborhood loved riding their bicycles. Our neighborhood was full of kids playing all sorts of games and doing all sorts of things. My sister had a girl bike where the bar was lowered. She hardly knew how to ride it at 4 years of age, but she tried. I was now 6-years old, and I too had a bike. It was my first bike, and it was a twin bike. It was a pretty blue bike with nice big wheels to press through all the dirt and mud I was used to driving through. It was great! It was my favorite toy of the day. It was like my own car. I rode my bicycle everywhere. I thought I was a pro on my bike. I would ride fast, and I would ride far, at least I thought it was far. I would go up hills and down hills and through other sections of the complex. I was learning my way around and my world was much bigger since I was not on foot anymore.

One day I had a flat. I was devastated and I needed some help. No one was around to help, so I went to my mother and asked her for help. She had a visitor at the time and his name was Joe. He was an older guy and he looked older than my mother. He was extremely nice. I was very eager to break into their conversation to ask if he could help me fix my bike as the chains had also fallen loose. He was eager to help, and my mom agreed.

Joe told me to come down with my bike to his apartment at the very end of the road and he would fix it right there on the spot. "Oh boy!!!" I was excited now. Joe left and headed home. I eventually followed with my bike to get it repaired so that I could get back on the road again. I took my bike down the street. I lifted the bike up the stairs to the front door of the apartments and then down to the basement apartment.

The apartment was to the left as I got to the end of the stairs. Though I had never gone inside, I knew where he lived because he was a friend of the family and Mom would visit him sometimes too. Joe invited me inside. When I entered the apartment, it was shaped exactly like our apartment. After entering his apartment, I saw a living room and through the living room, there was a nice place for a dining room table. The kitchen was to the left and the hallway to the bedrooms was along the right side of the apartment wall. There were three bedrooms and a bathroom through the hallway, though I had not seen those yet. I knew it was the same kind of apartment because we lived in the exact same layout except we were on the third floor and at the beginning of the section instead of the end like Joe.

He told me to put my bike near the television and have a seat. I did. I sat down and watched television. My bike slightly blocked the television, but I did not care. I was excited and eager to get it fixed.

Joe was in the back somewhere and I could hear him telling me, "I will be there soon!" Joe finally came out from the back and sat right beside me. I asked him, "can you fix my bike?" He said, "Give me one minute." I was confused as to why he was not hurrying. I wanted to get out there on the road to continue playing with the kids in the neighborhood. He kept switching the channels on the television and asked me if I wanted to watch something else and if I wanted something to drink. I said, "No, can you fix my bike?" That was all I wanted. He finally said, "I will fix your bike if you do something for me."

I would do anything for my bike. "Ok." I said, reluctantly, but eager to get things on the road again. He then pulled out his "thing" and asked me to put my mouth on it. I was scared and did not want to do that. I was so scared that I just wanted to go. He even put his hand on my head and tried to push my head down near his "thing." He said, "I can't fix your bike unless you do this for me." I was trapped. I wanted my bike fixed so badly and I felt like I had to give up something. It was like payment for the bike because he said that he would fix it for free. He said, "I want you to do something else. I will fix your bike and fix it anytime you need it fixed. I just want you to do this one thing and you can go after that and it won't take long." I agreed and he asked me to come in the back with him and sit on his bed.

I went into one of the bedrooms and sat on the bed. Everything was so neat back there. It was not like our house where kids lived, and everything could be all over the floor one day. Of course, my mother would beat us for it, but we would still mess up things. The bedroom door was open where I could see the hallway, the other bedroom and the bathroom. The bathroom door was opened, and he took off all his clothes. I could see him rubbing baby oil all over himself. I was frozen in my seat.

I did not know what he was doing. He came out of the room and told me that he would be here in one second. He went into the other bedroom and grabbed one of those huge multi-gallon spring water jugs that get delivered to your house. He was using it for a piggy bank. He had a lot of money in there. He brought it into the bedroom and dumped a lot of coins out on the bed beside me. He told me, "I will give you 500 pennies if you do what I say to do, ok?" I was terrified, but I knew he was going to fix my bike. He was my mother's good friend, and he was giving me some money, 500 pennies worth. I said, "Ok."

He put all the coins back in the huge piggy bank and then came around to me and took me off the bed. I stood there in front of him, and he took off all my clothes. He stripped me naked and put baby oil all over my body. He turned me on my stomach and laid me on the bed while the bed was still made. It was the most pain I ever felt in my little life.

I was screaming and screaming and crying. He just kept going. I was dying. After a while, he turned me over because I could not stop crying. He started to rub all over me and kept telling me to stop crying. I could not stop, it just hurt too much. I just lay there and just cried.

He was mad now. He got up from atop of me and went to get the piggy bank. He dumped the coins back on the bed and counted out pennies. He told me, "I'm not giving you 500 pennies. I'm only giving you 100 pennies since you cried so much." I did not care.

I just wanted to get out, so I took the 100 pennies and put them in the right pocket of my little shorts. My pocket was full of pennies and was bulging. He helped me put my clothes back on and he put his clothes back on and we both went to the living room where my bike was. I could not walk at all. I was so sore that I could not sit down. I stood near the bike to watch him fix it. He fixed the loose chains, and he fixed my flat tire. He told me, "This is between you and me, you better not tell nobody." I took my bike and walked out of the house.

I walked my bike to the local bowling alley around the back of the apartment complex to avoid anyone watching or seeing me. I could not ride my bike. The bowling alley is where we kids went to spend a little money on arcades and joke around. We would not even bowl. When I made it to the bowling alley, I parked my bike inside the bowling alley and went to the cash register and asked the worker for two quarters and a Coca-Cola.

She changed my 100 pennies. I went to the arcade machine and started playing a game. I was by myself. I just drank my Coca-Cola and played a couple of Ms. PacMan games. When I was finished, I went home. I still could not ride my bike. I went into the apartment, and no one was home except my father, and he was in the room asleep, I thought. I went to the bathroom, and I sat on the toilet. I was hurting so bad and when I looked in the toilet, I was bleeding. Blood was everywhere in the toilet. Blood was on my clothes, just everywhere. I did not tell anyone. I cleaned myself up and just shut my mouth. It was closed as far as I was concerned. I could never speak of it again. I must seal it forever. I was paid for it.

" *He told me,
this is between
you and me,
you better not
tell nobody.* "

DUKE ELLINGTON

The last semester of Langley Junior High was upon us and so was the audition to enter none other than the amazing Duke Ellington School of the Arts. I had heard of Duke Ellington through my eighth-grade music teacher, Ms. Pamela Alexander, as she had suggested it to me. Perhaps she thought I had a chance given my experience through the Playmakers and my obvious love for music and theater.

As my junior high school included ninth grade then, I had to wait two long years before nervously tracking down those same halls many greats have previously done, in the name of audition. Duke Ellington was simply a sight to behold. It was none other than a castle to me. It was gigantic and all white. It had sprawling steps and columns that reached the clouds. I looked up at the majestic building. I was in awe. I was intimidated. Like the audition for the Playmakers, Mama, being all that she could be to all of us, while working full time, could not make it, nor could anyone else. It had become the new normal for my siblings and I who sought activities outside the home to experience such a journey, solo. And so, it was for me that day. There was no Melvin this time. I held on to my nerves and trotted inside to meet my fate.

William, Mr. Know it all, what are you doing here? Are you out of your mind? This is no place for you.

Doubt became my garment. I was a stranger in a strange land who had to become a soldier in that strange land. An older woman–Ms. Dawn, appearing to be in the 40-50s age group, was my judge for that day. I was brought into a room with a black piano. She sat. I swallowed quickly. I prayed she did not see the nerves jumping around uncontrollably. Perhaps she did as not too long prior to seeing me, she was bellowing a wide range of notes before a class of students. As she did with her voice previously, she did it on the piano with varying scales, and indicated for me to accompany those scales with my voice. I guessed it went well and a few weeks later, an envelope came to Mama's house. Inside was an acceptance letter from Duke Ellington School of the Arts. I was thrilled.

There was more thrilling news. Mama had now secured her piece of the American Dream. It was the year 1989 and between the Home Purchasing Assistance Program (HPAP) and Mama knowing the seller of a house on Franklin Street, NE, D.C., she became a homeowner. Mama did not have much to accompany her to the new address, but she had her address to call home. She saved her money and worked toward a downpayment. My address went from the southeast side of D.C. to the northeast, residing again with Mama.

This meant the trek to Duke Ellington would be quite a distance by bus, and it was. To say the school was amazing would be an understatement. From my choir classes to learning to sing in Italian, German and French to learning voice, to projecting while speaking, and to be taught by renowned professionals was simply remarkable.

I had developed my voice and was performing in recitals. Though many loved my voice, this was not Langley. I was not the talent among those less interested in the arts. At Duke, it felt quite the opposite. Prolific singers, dancers, artists of all genres added to my insecurities. Similar to the Playmakers producing some of the finest in their crafts, so did Duke Ellington. There, two grades above me was a student named Dave Chapelle. There was also a young man named Tony Terry, who had come many years before me, and another named Raquis Da'Juan Petree with whom I bonded who started when I did. Many more went on the Broadway shows, musicals, graced Hollywood films and performed other acts. Diversity of artistry was not the only gold mine at Duke.

Learning that there were people across the world with varying ideas concerning God and spirituality—whether it was Buddhist or Nirvana—was fascinating. Being a Baptist Christian was not all there was, though it was all I knew. World Cultures course muddied the waters for me regarding my own walk of faith. Churches were to be staples of hope and inclusiveness; yet I experienced much judgment. Nevertheless, amazing people occupied the hallways of Duke Ellington and so did friends, at least, that was the term I used loosely. The glitz and glamor started to lose its shine. Things slowly started to become repeated unwanted episodes. Loneliness crept back into my arms.

"William is late again."

Being on time for class frequently escaped me. The stares from all eyes across the classrooms pounded upon me. Humiliation slapped me around and once again, craving the art of disappearance became a norm. The academics segment, such as biology and English–perhaps due to the structure–did little to complement my learning style. As such, the challenge wore me down and humiliation took center place. So, I did what I knew well. I channeled the clown in me and became a nuisance to teachers, administration and students. Such distractions did not distract Mr. Bryson from my failing grades. The 15-year-old sitting across from Mama and Mr. Bryson had lost his voice that day.

"William, do you have anything to say for yourself regarding your grades and the decision for the school to expel you? This is out of our hands."

I shrugged my shoulders. What could I say? How could I make them understand when I did not? I took my shrugged shoulders, my humiliation, my sense of nothingness, with the permanent dismissal from Duke Ellington School of the Arts and exited the grandeur of the white castle with Mama, looking back at my failed future. We entered the halls of Roosevelt High School. There, I excelled in varied things including FBLA-Future Business Leaders of America. There was no soprano, alto, or baritone echoing the halls. There were children at Powell, a nearby elementary school, that desperately needed a mentor, and I was asked to fill that role, working with latch key kids.

"William, would you mind sharing your story?" The guidance counselor asked one day, after learning that I had a story.

I did not know how to respond to the guidance counselor. I was not in an office with a therapist sitting across from me.

I obliged the guidance counselor who convinced the principal. I told my story in the school cafeteria that doubled as an auditorium. Sniffles and tears flooded the room. It was only when I exited the stage onto the playground, I realized how much support I had. As little bodies raced my way in an attempt to make impact with huge hugs, I felt the power of one's testimony upon another. I did not realize how important that was to kids who were living in communities impacted with compounded trauma of violence upon violence. I even developed a bond with my very own mentee from school. Nonetheless, Roosevelt too was a challenge. After that dismissal, came a residential treatment in the Commonwealth of Pennsylvania.

THE LONE RESIDENT

I was not a stranger to Pennsylvania. Visiting my cousin and her daughter and son were always fond experiences. They were amongst the most fun folks I have ever known. Their religion, though, seemed to have made them live differently from the rest of us in the family. They identified as Jehovah's Witnesses, and they were always kind and fun. So, I anticipated Pennsylvania being a fun place, though it would not be at my cousin's. I did not know how long it was going to be before I saw my siblings again. The day before we left for Pennsylvania was a time as good as any to say my goodbyes.

Nicci, my younger sister, was living across town with my other family members. The only way for me to get to her was by car. Mama's car then became the object of my desire. Thus, I secretly borrowed it.

One of my friends came along with me for the ride. On our way back, I crossed an intersection a few miles away from home. As I crossed the light, a driver of a small sports car, however, was driving at top speed and sped through his red light at the same intersection.

I turned immediately to the steering wheel, tucked into it, held it tightly so it could not breath and waited for the impact. The other driver smashed into the back left driver side of the two-door car and the car went around in circles like a marble that was just spun. The other car hit us so hard that I literally fell into the other seat with my friend.

I immediately got out of the car and realized that our rear axle was on the ground and the right passenger rear wheel was making its way down North Capitol Street with no stopping in sight. I yelled at the other driver profusely. When I heard sirens, I immediately jumped back in the car to allow for the medics to examine me. The ambulance took me to the hospital. Routine tests were conducted and then my doctor released me in the silent hours of the morning. The paramedics graciously gave me a ride back home in the ambulance. I crawled in bed as if nothing happened.

When Mama awakened, she asked me if I had seen her car. Without details, I told her I had borrowed the car and there was an accident. As to be expected, her voice hit the high pitch range and the house trembled. She contacted her insurance company, and the agent completed the puzzle for her. I sat in my humiliation all morning pretending to be tired and sleep. A rental car joined us for Pennsylvania. The silence in the car was deafening. Her silently fuming made me want to temporarily lose my sight. When we arrived at the treatment facility, we both could not have been more relieved. Despite her head dropping, I knew Mama wanted more than anything some sort of help for me to get me through the nightmare I was living.

The grounds of the facility were beautiful. The campus had different houses and places for activities-- baseball fields, indoor basketball and varied cottages. Then just like that, the beauty faded. I was housed in the main housing facility where youth who were in need of more acute care were placed. I was instantly categorized as an arms-length resident and was placed on a one-to-one (1:1) watch.

For hours, days, weeks, and months, my shadow and another human were always with me. I sat in class, and so did the other human. I went to the restroom, and so did the other human. I went into my bedroom, and so the other human sat by my door all night. Mama did not tell me I was coming to a prison. Like one tucked away from those in the general population, I could only watch as other residents ran, walked, and played freely throughout the campus. What was happening to me? Why was I being punished? What did I do?

I remembered the bridge in D.C. I remembered wanting to jump off that bridge. Was that the reason? Many viewed me as having a teenage identity crisis. Upon their belief, there was a shift in energy. Without words being spoken, their changed behavior or passive aggressive attitude made me feel as if I were in solitary confinement. Was that the reason? I thought to myself, okay, whatever the reasons, every problem has a solution so how was I going to resolve this problem and make the authorities believe I was not who they thought me to be?

I learned that there were point systems and points were earned based on trust. My desired achievement was to gain enough trust based on my behavior. I would have the privilege of only 15 minutes check time as opposed to 24 hours 1:1. That would be a huge accomplishment for me. I conquered it somehow and I was now living in the cottage away from the main house. I had friends and I was loving it. I then felt the sudden brakes on my new, found "freedom." Someone stole from the cottage. More devastating was the culprit was not forthcoming. Just like that, my 15 minutes was revoked, and I was placed back on arms-length.

Tension brewed in the cottage. I was the most restricted so their step down was maybe they could not play games or no trips but my step down was heading back to the main facility, up the hill.

I had grown tired from these 1:1s. They were disrespectful, offensive and I felt that I was a man now. Folks had started to form their own cliques and I was the great lone wolf with my permanent shadow in the form of a human being.

So, a couple of guys and I made the daring decision to exercise our "rights," and chose our right to refuse treatment. We signed the Against Medical Advice Form and as custom dictated, we were placed in 72-hour isolation. In isolation, and to avoid influencing other residents, the facility thought it was best for there to be zero communication with others, and not even the bathroom was shared with others at the same time. The food was brought to our rooms, and I even ate alone. One of the guys signed back on after 48 hours, but no, not me. The other teen resident and I did our 72 hours like champions, gladly received the cash from our account, accepted the ride from the facility to the train station bound for Philadelphia and connected to a Greyhound bus–destination–Washington D.C.

PART II

Reflections

So many years I had held on to that tiny slither of hope for a brand-new start — a start that would get rid of the feelings of defeat, anger, prolonged sadness, and what Mama called, "...living a suicidal lifestyle."

Therapy helped tremendously but I did not realize early on that these were seeds for a monumental shift in my attitude, future actions, and attempts to strengthen my self-esteem and rebuild my dignity. It was a long walk in my own shoes.

Our entire family, Mama, my siblings – uncles, aunts, cousins, and those who knew and loved Mom and Tony were all traumatized by the events of the past. We were all trying to find a way to survive – forget thriving. I was learning how to be less anxious and had some therapeutic tools under my belt including learning how to communicate with others in an entirely different way. I learned what it meant to be assertive, aggressive, passive, and direct. Deploying these tools would not come easy, but it was a start.

The inner advocate began to advocate for me. I packed my bags, and I began the journey of an adult, albeit way sooner than I wanted. I was not sure where I was headed, and it did not matter.

It was time for me to be the one.

PART III
Circle of Healing

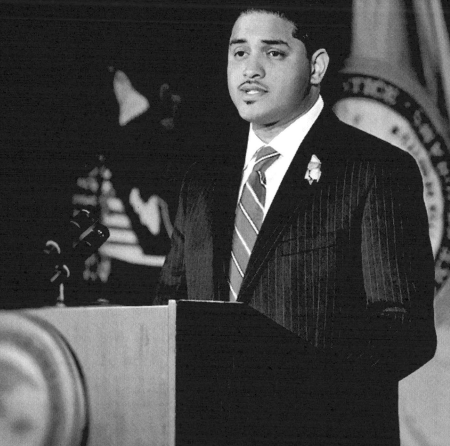

William shares his story of resilience as the guest keynote speaker at the National Candlelight Observance, hosted by the Office for Victims of Crime during National Crime Victims' Rights Week, 2010.

Photo: Courtesy of the U.S. Department of Justice

GENERAL EQUIVALENCY

I eventually landed back at Mama's place. Confusion, worry, frustration, lack of knowledge wore on me. I have to do something with my life. Mama never mentioned her feelings toward my leaving Pennsylvania. I knew that my actions had to prove something differently than what Mama may have believed— that I had made the wrong decision to leave Pennsylvania. Living my life as it was, hurt me more. I was determined. My tomorrows had to be brighter than my yesterdays. I did not know the demons that were awaiting me before that moment could occur.

I could not get a high school diploma from Duke Ellington, but I could get something equivalent to a high school diploma. The General Equivalency Diploma (G.E.D.) exam was my next stop. It was the only door that would allow me to enter other chapters of my life—job, college, I thought. I signed up for the test. With fear as my companion, we showed up for the test. I was not alone. Approximately 100 people who sat in that huge room had to also do something with their lives. I followed the instructions to the different parts of the test and showed up as instructed two weeks later to learn my destiny that was predetermined by this test. I went

93

back to that same place, and I went to the counter, spoke to the receptionist and requested the results.

"You exhibited some challenges in math, but congratulations, you earned your G.E.D."

"Wow!" I caught myself from falling from excitement.

"Wait for about 20 minutes, and we will get the diploma to you."

Wait! Is she kidding me?! I had to figure out my next plan. What was I going to do? Well certainly, I had to rock N roll. And I did, with the help of a friend, I rolled into my first job at Lulu's New Orleans Cafe owned by the Augers, who also owned a first class, high-end fine dining restaurant in Washington D.C., patronized by the likes of U.S. presidents, senators, and the crème de la crème in Washington, D.C.–Blackie's House of Beef.

My duty at Lulu's New Orleans Café was to be a host. What was that? I have never worked in a restaurant business before, but I did gain experience at 14 years old working for the Marion Barry Summer Youth Employment Program, for about three years making as little as $3 an hour. I took my SYEP training and grabbed discipline and got to work. Where was the library? What are the duties and responsibilities of a host? How do you master techniques such as welcoming customers into the establishment? How do you make them feel special? Oh, this is familiar. Like the Playmakers, I am performing. I was good at that. As such, I performed and grabbed the attention of the general manager and a floor supervisory position grabbed me in just three months.

I must have thought Mom was with me one day while I headed to work. I realized quickly this was not elementary school, and the person in charge was not going to look the other way while I was the last to make an entrance. Being late was not on the menu and my boss in no uncertain terms made that very clear to me. With shame whipping me, I ensured being late from thereon stayed off the menu. It worked as I was later promoted to the manager of the establishment six months later. This was only the beginning of my restaurant experience.

Despite silent tears from Mom on her birthday, I sang a loud happy birthday for customers of theirs at a new restaurant, just as the general manager did before me. I sang my way into Phillips Flagship Restaurant, where due to my performance, I was encouraged to audition for "Rent," the Broadway musical written by Jonathan Larson, by a long-time friend who knew of my talents.

I had not heard of Rent, or its soundtrack. During my audition, I caught the attention of one who worked at WOL Radio in Washington, D.C. who invited me to have a conversation on her show about the path that landed me on my audition. To my surprise, Channel 8, an ABC affiliate, visited the restaurant to document my conversation and experience. There were talks of me heading to the Great White Way as a natural next step. The Great White Way? What was that? I did my research and discovered that it was a nickname for a section of Broadway in the Midtown section of New York City, between 42nd and 53rd Streets that encompasses the Theatre District. I was instantly on high.

Theatre District! Are you kidding me? I could be on stage all over again. How fast could I get there? In no time, I was looking out from beyond a stage on Broadway performing for an opportunity to be cast in "Rent." I kept looking for a call back after at least four call backs in a row, but there was none. I was then looking out from beyond a stage on Broadway performing for an opportunity to be cast for The Lion King. I kept looking for a call back but there was none. My spirit slumped. I knew this feeling. Rejection was no stranger to my doorsteps.

There was one place I learned where I would feel welcomed. It was a family I thought I had not yet known but who would embrace me passionately. It is one of the few places where I did not have to be on stage or perform.

"*I have to do something with my life.*"

FIREBIRDS

School and I were at our "catch me if you can" game again. I did not catch it at Duke Ellington. I did not catch it at Roosevelt. Certainly, I would catch it at the University of the District of Columbia, home of the Firebirds. It had been about a decade now of building my skills in the restaurant industry, and surely, I knew the rules of the game. At least that is what I thought until nothing materialized from my application. Nope. I was going to win this game this time around.

After what seemed like hours of standing on that financial aid line, doubt and jitters assured me that I was not alone, hence, we left together. We did not make it all the way because I escaped them one day and went back on that line. I had closed the entry door for doubt and jitters to access me, and as a result, a financial aid counselor opened his office door allowing me to enter. Like the G.E.D. tests had revealed, so did my placement test at the university—I needed a refresher in math and English courses. And so, it was.

In Spring 2003, I was a student of higher learning. Naturally, as a performer, I leaned toward a communications degree given that I wanted to be a television producer. That was until I remembered that at one time, I wanted to heal the sick with an M.D. affixed to my person; so, I enrolled in the pre-med program pursuing biology, making it to my junior year. I traded in my white lab coat and continued to wear my suits to business classes. The dean of the business school became my official guide. The School of Business and Public Administration was popping on campus and its larger-than-life self was so attractive that its magnet pulled me back to my innermost desire of entrepreneurship. My game walk would now take place as a future candidate for the Baccalaureate Degree in Business Management. I was ready.

In Fall 2004, I had joined another line and at the end of it, was the embrace from other colors. The blue and white from Phi Beta Sigma Fraternity, Incorporated, had taken my soon to be brothers from three to thousands. I was from the Gamma Lambda Chapter. I had a pep in my step.

I stepped into election fever the following semester and chose the only healing remedy for the students I saw. I cast my vote. Representing the business school, I draped my suit and tie, and as a good citizen went to introduce myself to my new undergraduate student government president. When I arrived at her office, the young man who had occupied the presidential chair informed me that the elected president would not be sworn into her duties, as something occurred preventing her from taking the position and that I was now looking at the new president.

"In what ways may I serve you and our students Mr. President Bernard Marion Grayson, Jr.?"

And just like that, I was a member of the Student Government's Student Services Committee, which centered around student needs. Like LuLu's New Orleans Café, my work was evident of my excitement and passion. Like LuLu's New Orleans Café, it allowed me to shake hands with promotion and I was now promoting students' agendas as the chief of staff for the Undergraduate Student Government Association President. Little did I know that another promotion was peeking its head from around the corner. It was pushed all the way around when the Association's rules caused the secretary of the Student Government Association to be ousted based on the lack of meeting attendance. And with the stroke of a pen, I was now the secretary.

And for our hard work as part of the executive body, the University thanked us immensely by offering us free tuition. As I was now on campus full-time, this worked for me. I was really playing this "catch me if you can" game. Dr. Clemmie Solomon, vice president of student affairs lifted previous student government administration restrictions which allowed us to begin flourishing as student leaders. Semesters later, I was fully groomed to run for the current president's position, as President Grayson's term had come to an end. We congratulated him on his graduation, and he congratulated me on my presidency win, with the smartest guy around as my vice president—Eric Broussard-Bueno. I was not only playing this game; I was winning. My role as a president would quickly teach me that seeing the seat and working for the one in the seat was not the same as sitting in the seat. The game has now been intensified. It was my move. With my first speech in hand, co-written by Selvon Waldron, my deputy chief of staff, nothing could stop me from serving the student body.

> "The game has now been intensified. It was my move."

MR. PRESIDENT

As I walked the halls of the University of the District of Columbia, the name William Kellibrew became a university-wide name. Whether it was the custodian, the president of the university or the chair of the board of trustees, the role as president of the USGA brought with it a certain level of prestige, access, responsibility and accountability. My role as a natural performer brought to the position a certain flair. The summer retreat with my team invoked confidence in me to carry out our agenda, largely thanks to Ms. Mary Roberts. My role as a problem fixer and people pleaser, often-times transformed my office into an overnight guest room with me as the guest. Entertaining was second nature to me, so on campus, I stayed on task as a host. Lulu's New Orleans Café had taught me well. Suit and tie were my daily attire of choice; so was my smile.

"Hello, how are you?"

"Good to see you."

"Yes, let's do lunch some time."

Those refund checks from financial aid, given my full tuition paid, had me living among the clouds. I rode those clouds into my recreational time playing tennis. However, to the coach, based on my technique and athleticism, my riding became business. I was now offered free on-campus housing and a full scholarship as a member of the UDC tennis team.

Life could not be better. I was invited to join the Honda All Star Team Challenge, a quiz bowl academic competition for Historically Black Colleges and Universities held in Orlando, with free tickets to Disney World. That guaranteed me an "A" automatically in a public speaking course. I needed it. My campus-celebrity status was only able to move some in the classroom, not all. A grade of "D" in marketing that warranted a repeat was a game changer. I was transforming into that secretary-missing meetings held in a classroom with academics as the agenda. Nonetheless, I was not her. I was going to stay in position, on cloud 11.

Occasionally, I would look down. Wearing the University's burgundy blazer, I strutted across the campus plaza, in and out of offices, in and out of classrooms, commanded audiences, ignited a revolution championing students' rights. I was present and I was center stage. That center stage emulated itself on the cover of BusinessWeek. I never looked sharper.

Though on this new stage, many saw me; still, they did not see me. That would not be for long as everything in the dark must eventually come to light. My presidency brought me to many doors, and one day, it did to that of the director of communications. I could not say precisely what it was about the director, but he provided a light space in which communication could find peace. And so, it did.

Without struggle, the door to the secret room slowly was ajar. Light seeped inside and the secret of that deadly morning of July 2nd, 1984—Mom, Tony, Marcus fell out at the director's feet. Apparently, he had no intentions of creating another room for it; so, when he learned that "America's Dad," was going to visit our campus house, and the panel upon which he was going to sit was in need of a student with a unique story, the director was now at my door.

Sharing the stage with elite members of our community,

chief of police, forensic pathologists, other community representatives and that famous dad, Bill Cosby, was surreal. There were
at least 1000 people in the audience including Mama. The musical
chair began, and it was my turn to tell my story. I was now forced
to stand. Where was Lulu's New Orleans Café training now? Where
was the host when you needed him? Nerves grappled me. My student
government family. Students. Professors. Custodians. All the
speakers of the household name were silent. What could I possibly
have to add to the stories of this esteemed group of panelists?

With frailty shaking me, I uttered words. The L shaped
object. The red. The cries of mercy. As I told of that dreadful
morning, I could see the ears of "America's Dad," piqued. As I spoke,
they piqued more and more. I could hear the sounds of Mama ...
one hour ... where's my child ... two hours ... where's my child ... three
hours gone by ... where's my child.

"For at least three hours, Mama thought her daughter was
alive. For at least three hours, I knew her daughter had died."

The stronghold of agony had gripped me so tightly, there
was no escaping it. The flood of tears could not have carried me
away. I managed to point to the woman who had been searching
for her daughter. She stood. I know to others her standing was to
set her apart so they could see her. For me, it was another reminder
that she saw me. The entire audience stood and surrounded her
with a mighty applause. The secret room was on TV One Station's
screen. The secret room was now in the room of many viewers.

"The entire audience stood and surrounded her with a mighty applause."

SUNDERLAND

Frenzy had decided to pay the University of the District of Columbia a visit. The student who is our student president. Our student president was a victim of crime. A victim of crime who had caught the attention of Bill Cosby and a TV One producer. Whispers chatted.

> *Is he 20, is he 25, is he 30? He looks so young. How could he have survived all that? Is he okay? He is on the tennis team. He is always taking care of everybody around here. He sleeps in his office. Why didn't he say something?*

While the whispers made their way around, a call made its way to me. The Washington Post newspaper outlet in Washington DC wanted to create a special on me. And they did. My sun would shortly dim. Another of my loved ones—gone too soon. Ten stabs... twenty stabs...thirty stabs ... fifty stabs. At the hands of an ex-boyfriend, my god sister, while under U.S. Marshall's protection was murdered. From her death, my advocacy targeting domestic violence was birthed. My family, close friends and I started a campaign against this atrocity and continued the capturing of audiences. This time, it was the Washington Post. As love is magnetic, it drew two professors at the university to create the William Kellibrew Foundation. Wow! I felt like dancing ... like that 15-year-old, 5 feet 4, light-skinned, red-boned firecracker that had everyone's attention on the dancing floor.

I was still entrenched in my presidential role and was tasked with selecting a student to represent the District of Columbia to attend the University in Sunderland, England as an educational exchange. As I had failed to solidify a student, the presidential thing to do was simply to take on the task, and so I agreed, upon request from Clarence Davis and other professors in the College of Arts and Sciences. At the sending off party, I learned quickly that it was a different kind of party. There was a jazz band, well set tables, city administrators including Secretary of the City, the University President, Mr. William Pollard, and another student representative, but from George Washington University. The public and a private university were sending representatives to the District's sister school based on an agreement of exchange based on culture, economics and education. We were the education part of the agreement.

Flavors similar to the sounds of Ms. Pierre flooded me. Smiles carried me and landed me at BBC Worldwide. I thought it was odd and wondered how the purpose of my study abroad expanded from student to celebrity.

"So you are that American guy....and you ran for student government and you....?"

Sometimes, I looked forward to just being in my flat shared by four other students. My escape also involved tennis. History carried itself to the present and I caught the attention of the tennis coach. I was now a member of the University of Sunderland Tennis team—in the first team with three top tennis players—Gareth, Paul and Pottsy with Andy as our honorary member. All sports had several teams made up of four players with our team at the top. I looked forward to Wednesdays.

On that designated sports day, all 60+ teams would go out and play other teams across the country in our respective sports. At the end of the day, we would all break bread over laughter and stories. Sensation was so addictive that one of the professors held a TED Talk based on me, entitled, "The Power of Community." The city leader of Sunderland presented the other student from George Washington and me with a lifetime position of being a Sunderland ambassador. Together, we were the 94th worldwide ambassadors for the Sunderland City Council. I spoke throughout the city, in schools, to youth offenders, the youth parliament, city agencies and others.

Ambassadors also get a chance to attend many of the events hosted by the Sunderland City Council, Mayor and other dignitaries. This was a great chance to get to meet others in the city and to hang out with my amazing Sunderland government hosts, Catherine and Tom. This one particular event, hosted annually, is at the Sunderland Museum and Winter Gardens, which is a tropical paradise. The museum featured a Scenic Lift to the Treetop Walkway and over 2,000 plants in the glass rotunda. With my invitation in hand, along with my god-brother Thomas "Tommy" Slack, from Edinburgh, Scotland, who doubled as my photographer, sat quietly, and spellbound at our table seated next to another ambassador—an avid famous mountain climber, another ambassador—a locally famous businessman and the list goes on. The experience was positively overwhelming.

Later, having a moment to myself at my flat, I checked my newly established Yahoo email account.

"Dear William,

....

Signed,

Harpo Entertainment."

Wow! I know this name! I have heard of its CEO! With her

came a dressing room, car service. Imagine how floored I was when I spoke to one of the producers at HARPO Studios. Being on the Oprah Winfrey Show could catapult me into a world unknown. Bill Cosby was not far from view as he was the bridge that connected us. As high as that made me feel, I was quickly brought back to a low when I revisited that dreadful morning, the place into which I last heard my mother's cry. Endless times prior to that moment, I had returned to the neighborhood, never to the house. I had run away a few times but ran past that house. Fear prohibited me from going; yet, here I was, at the invitation of Oprah. I had brought three others on the show with me. As usual and deservingly, Mama received yet another standing ovation.

When I returned to the University, I received a hero's welcome from the University of Sunderland, the Sunderland City Council and newly acquainted friends. I presented the Sunderland City Council and Mayor with one of the gifts from the Oprah Show. I was placed to stand in the same location as Her Majesty the Queen, Elizabeth II, whenever she presented her gifts to the city—and there were many. Tears blinded me as my gift was placed in the Mayor's Parlor in the same casings as Her Majesty's gifts. Celebration carried itself to the roof tops.

Back at the University in the theater that seated at least 102 people facing a big screen with my classmates, tennis mates, professors, city council leaders, Sunderland University administrators, like any other fan of William, I excitedly sat down to watch the Oprah Show. The kid who ran from bullies, had hopelessness tightly tucked away in his backpack as he stood on that bridge, who paid a price for his innocence to be violently stolen from him was now an international figure of hope and resilience. The thorns within the rose were becoming less visible. All the while, celebrations at the University of the District of Columbia, back in the United States ramped up with the school holding a reception and professors grabbing extra televisions to showcase the story in classrooms. I called in the day the Oprah Winfrey Show aired to show my love and support to students, faculty and staff who watched as I laid my soul bare. I was devastated to find that with Bill Cosby's conviction, I was compelled to distance myself and my work. Even the appearance and then the conviction placed me in a very awkward position to even discuss my association. I stopped but was intent to simply lay out the facts in this memoir – account of my truth and my story.

"The kid who ran
from bullies,
had hopelessness tightly
tucked away in his backpack
as he stood on that bridge,
who paid a price
for his innocence to be
violently stolen from him
was now an
international figure
of hope and resilience."

GAME CHANGER

I longed for the sister city. I was back in America. Still, the roars from the Stadium of Light where Sunderland AFC Football Team exhibited greatness, deafened me. As an ambassador, opportunities and events called me, from formal seemingly posh events to speaking opportunities with youth. Among those was the privilege to watch a football match in the Stadium of Light. This privilege brought with it a suite from which to enjoy the games. Within that suite were about another hundred privileged souls. We were treated like Greek gods. Suit and tie only. Dinner served in an opulence ambiance. No expression of joy, such as clapping for your team, much less a roar. Those were for the other souls—not in the suites. Those souls were wild. Those souls' voices and stomping rocked the earth, "boom boom boom...red and white army. Boom boom boom...red and white army."

Red wine filled the spaces in the air, and bodies pound on each other from the jilt of excitement. "Boom boom boom...red and white army." Who wanted all that fuss when I had the rare opportunity to control my urges on wanting to scream, "Go Sunderland!" Why clap when I could be poised? I smiled when I remembered the place called Sunderland. Her people. Their ways. No tracksuit in a pub. One's tennis shoes were not invited at all venues. Do not forget one's jacket at home. If one were caught in such attire, as I often was, well one simply was not—well, classy enough or could not enter. My cheeks widened and my eyes lit when I thought of my sister city and her ways. They were not so different from our ways here in America, in many respects.

Sunderland must have known I was trapped in time as she called me back using my tennis team family at the university as her channel. The city-wide competition among universities for all the sports—scuba diving, tennis, etc. had called for champions to defend their titles and new ones to be birthed. In no time, I headed to the call of my new family and landed back in England. We fought and fought and fought hard and did not fight showing off the winning trophy. We were among the champions that were birthed that year. The celebration dinner was no short of being spectacular, neither was the welcome back home in America.

The excitement quickly fizzled. I was back in the states and there was a new president of the University of the District of Columbia and he had declared war on its comrades and had decided to raise the tuition more than 100%. I was still dripping from the wetness of being an international student at Sunderland, so I immediately thought of the impact on our international students, who had already secured a predetermined budget that, if slightly shaken, could change the trajectory of their lives. Not on my watch.

As most things standing fall when the foundation is moved, a few students and I with bull horns started to create a crack in the president's agenda. For weeks, erected tents and unwanted overnight student guests plagued the Green Space on campus. That plague spread to the front of the campus, to around the campus. Night after night after night. Supporters brought us food. They brought us water. They brought us heat to battle the cold. We showed the City Council and the Mayor's Office the same signs we showed our

President. They heard the same sounds as we chanted in the city that I represented not too long ago across the Atlantic Ocean. The crack was getting wider, and the agenda was tilting.

"Mr. Kellibrew, the President of the university would like to make a deal."

I followed the President's attorney to my office and joined the President over the phone. Tuition would increase 25%, and steadily increase in increments, but eventually, it would hit 100%. Students would now have time to grapple and plan ahead for the expected change, as opposed to a sudden jolt. Something within had decided to leave me. I no longer had a desire to remain at the University. I was now the senior class president. So what? I was in my graduation year. So what? I was working for the National Coalition on Black Civic Engagement. So what? I had met with the mayor's people, the City Council President, and other prominent councilmen. Our demands were heard and were being met. So what? Something inside me had died and there was no awakening. I withdrew from the University of the District of Columbia. They had won the game. I had lost respect for the institution but kept the firebird spirit alive inside.

" *Not on my watch.* "

SISTER

The saying that history repeats itself laid at the feet of my heart. The irony with history is that it makes a noise so one is aware of its coming; yet, when it arrives, one is oftentimes astonished. As is customary in African American culture, I had a family member, in this case, a sister, who was not a sister by blood, not by legal adoption, but by the closeness of the relationship with the family -- closest to Nicci, my biological sister.

In our culture, it is nothing for us to open our doors to someone, we then share the same address; we eat the same food, we take on each other's issues, we are family. Their children and our children are family until someone discovers that they are not "family." By that time, it is too late because the mind has been transformed and cannot be convinced otherwise. The newest sister in my family had some struggles that were too close to home. An abusive boyfriend. An abusive boyfriend attempted to set her place on fire. An abusive boyfriend who was jailed. A jailhouse release to a halfway house stay. A sister who received a restraining order and was under the protection of the United States Government—the U.S. Marshall Service. A threatening phone message to my sister's apartment. A breaking into that apartment building and to that apartment. Cries for help.

Instead of an L shaped object, the weapon of choice was an elongated sharp object—stabs, not once, not twice, but fifty times. Death laid on the floor. This time its delivery man was captured alive. Blood has again stained the journey of my family. Two murdered by men that were to protect them. History did not promise kindness, but only a return. I could not do anything about Mom and Tony. I could do something about my sister.

A new vigor erupted within me. Without my knowledge, two professors, Clarence Davis and Barbara Harvey founded The William Kellibrew Foundation granting aid to students to support their education and now had evolved to address living in the web of domestic violence.

As I was already used to erecting tents and being the unwanted overnight guests on government premises, I thought why not continue the trend? Pavements—be it in cold, rain, sleet, snow—became home base in front of Washington D.C. City Hall and courts. Sleeping bags and blankets lined the pavement. The system was to protect my sister from the death dealer. How did he get past the U.S. Marshall? Where was the disconnect with communication? Someone would hear us. This violence in our community must garner attention. And it did.

The Washington Post heard us. There were calls for a registry of domestic abusers, but politics rose its head and that registry stayed a call. There was a call from Mildred Muhammad, Global Domestic Violence speaker, in forming a victim survivor alliance. There was a visit from United States Congressman John Lewis, a visit from Melanie Campbell, chief executive officer and president of the National Coalition on Black Civic Participation, a visit from Colin Goddard, Virginia Tech mass shooting survivor, and Tommy Slack, who rallied supporters in Edinburgh, Scotland, Brandon Wallace, Esq., then, executive director, among many other supporters.

I decided to make my call through awareness and educating people about domestic violence. I made my presence felt and demanded to be heard in this arena. As I fought to be heard in arenas, the William Kellibrew Foundation kept its movement in the streets. The president of the Brady Campaign to Prevent Gun Violence, which focused on combating gun violence, opened its doors and made the William Kellibrew Foundation family, sharing a space and resources. It was important to our executive director, Brandon J. Wallace, that we kept our focus on the issues and not the partisan politics. Working moms who were formerly incarcerated and later became public assistance recipients were able to volunteer with us and later be hired with many companies. More family. As they gain more skills, they transform their lives—new world travelers, new jobs gained.

The Foundation began to grow tentacles. It joined the District of Columbia Coalition Against Domestic Violence (DC-CADV), and the District of Columbia Victims Assistance Network. The community served by the Foundation grew from local to national. I started to grow tentacles. I was once asked to speak briefly at an event at a church and those words landed on the acting director for the Office for Victims Services with the U.S. Department of Justice, who became a mentor, and as such, invited me to different events.

As Joye Frost's eventual self-proclaimed mentee, she knew me well, and she thought that I would be a great speaker at the Office for Victims of Crimes' National Candlelight Observance in order to recognize and acknowledge and support victims and survivors of crime. With such privilege, came my face being depicted as the main speaker on a flier from the Department of Justice and being dispatched to over 12,000 post offices and beyond. As I sat in the Green Room, U.S. Attorney General Eric Holder appeared.

I walked up to him, we chatted and exchanged a joke. Shortly thereafter, we became sitting neighbors on stage. My mentor continued to catapult me—this time it was into the National Victims

Assistance Academy where I joined the Advanced Trainer Institute. There I learned techniques on how to speak. Many speaking engagements thereafter knocked on my door and their zip codes were from all over the country and world. As a boy, I would continuously take the scenic, adventurous and scary route through the woods for many miles just to avoid James the bully. Now, I enjoy the adventurous, scenic routes to speak against bullying.

My recognition in victim services and civic engagement catapulted me to a promotion at my work at the National Coalition on Black Civic Participation. I was the new deputy director and national victims' advocate.

CIVIC ENGAGEMENT

For one to arrive at a particular destination, there were several bridges that had to be crossed. When I was enjoying my service as student government president, I came upon a bridge that would later show me that the same kid that was held down and beaten by his elder family member for foul language would be the same man whose words would shape the narrative of the most powerful country on earth.

As was protocol, anyone that sought to engage the student government had to engage its President and, as such, Ms. Frederick reached out to me. We began working on a smoking cessation project with the Congressional Black Caucus. We worked well together. Our team effort was successful. And then just like that, she disappeared. Years later, during the second term of President George Bush, Ms. Frederick reappeared like magic.

She invited me to a conference, which I attended, as well as a workshop called, "Black Youth Vote." My contribution must have been noteworthy because it led Ms. Frederick to recommend a job to me at the National Coalition on Black Civic Participation, an organization formed in the 1970s by the National Association for the Advancement of Colored People or the NAACP, and the National Council of Negro Women, headed by Dr. Dorothy Irene Height. Dr. Height was chair emeritus and Ms. Melanie Campbell was the president and chief executive officer. The role involved traveling and engaging in activities that I thoroughly enjoyed, as well as learning about the bigger reach of the organization into civil rights matters, were more than I could have ever hoped.

As the job placed me into a spotlight drawing more eyes upon me, the passion of my advocacy caught the eye of one named Melanie. Consequently, I was offered the position of deputy director and national victims advocate and elatedly accepted her offer. Little William who starved for a sense of belonging among his peers was now being asked from different angles to join others in their circles. Life has a way of humbling those who live it. One of the tasks afforded to me was to become one of the youth point persons to vie for what could be a law passed in Congress called the American Affordable Care Act. This all depended on whether a new president and congress would have made that possible.

Being one of the point persons to get out the youth vote, I traveled with many of my non-partisan colleagues across 15 cities on the Walk Across America Tour with Bow Wow, planned and implemented by music mogul and executive, Michael T. Mauldin, Bow Wow, myself, and many others. We met with celebrities and anyone else having an impact on the youth to help garner a turn out never before seen. Apparently, it worked as a new president was named, President Barack Obama. As deputy director, I had to engage the White House as well as attend many meetings there including with special assistants to the President, and meetings at the Capitol with House and Senate Representatives. Once at one of my meetings in the Roosevelt Room, a room in the White House adjacent to the Oval Office, representing my organization along with Ms. Campbell; the task from the President's speech writer was for us to give thoughts based on the pulse of the people and what they needed regarding domestic economic policy. This was one of the many times I felt overwhelmingly, my impact, given my role as an advocate. I began to read from my notes.

"The President needs a blueprint from which people can build from their loss across the country, especially given the foreclosure crisis that happened in the early areas of the administration. The exodus from the suburbs in Detroit due to foreclosure to the exodus from Katrina."

I talked about this idea of stagnant upward mobility which was a quote from a New York Times article that was published and ironically seen by me earlier that day. The speech writer asked me for a copy of my notes, and I submitted them and went on my way. Couple nights later, the President was talking about giving the State of the Union address. A woman who had attended the meeting hastily called me and asked me to watch. I scurried to watch the program. It was as if all oxygen had left my body and I was paralyzed in disbelief. It was not because everyone in the class was staring at me because Mom was running late again, and I wanted to disappear into a cocoon.

Rather, the President of the United States of America had just adopted this idea of a blueprint and wrapped around his four pillars of American values. The President was intending to use my quote. My idea was used to frame the third State of the Union address of the Obama Administration. Wow ... so this was the destination of the bridge that was Ms. Frederick. A nation's agenda shaped from the idea of an American kid who lived in the Nation's Capital, leaned over another bridge, and decided to cross it as opposed to jumping from it.

My passion for civic engagement led me to speaking across the United States and the globe. Departing the Coalition was difficult but starting my speaking career full time as an entrepreneur would further give me purpose.

After moderating a scholarship ball program hosted by my

former local chapter, Alpha Sigma of Phi Beta Sigma Fraternity, Inc., a fraternity brother, Jeremy, asked if I was interested in connecting with an organization, the National Association of State Mental Health Program Directors and speaking at their National Summit.

I was overjoyed to be invited by Dr. Joan Gillece to share my story of childhood trauma and how I survived. "Welcome to our National Summit as part of the Substance Abuse and Mental Health Services Administration's National Center for Trauma-Informed Care. Please welcome a new friend and peer, William Kellibrew!" said Dr. Gillece. Over 40 states, countless counties, cities, organizations, agencies, and programs, my story was slowly making a difference in the lives of those we trained and supported. Receiving SAMHSA's Peer Leadership Award in Hollywood, California reminded me of the long journey of healing. Submitting my name for one of the highest honors in the United States on mental health had me pinching myself. Dr. Gillece had recognized my contributions and submitted my name for the award. I asked myself a million times, how did I make it here.

THE THERAPIST

The bridge outside the room awaits me. As I looked around the room, black gowns adorned with tassels draped many happy bodies. We did not know each other as our courses were online, but we knew each other as our journey to the completion of the baccalaureate degree in business administration at the University of Maryland Global Campus was similar to some extent.

Managing an office within the City of Baltimore's Department of Health in the day, and school papers at night may have been my journey; another could have mothering or fathering children in the household in the day, taking exams at night.

Either way, we had a similar story of sacrifice, of commitment, of discipline, of victory. I looked around and my soul smiled. I could see Mom dancing and Tony smiling. I saw Lorraine as she strutted across campus, as I remembered everything that she read to me, and I saw Dad as I ran into his arms when he arrived from the Big House. I saw my godfather as he took me in, in my desperate need for housing, and I felt the love of a grandfather gone too soon. The sneaking in and out of basements for ice cream and the screams of names when I was busy being a child. The memories that rushed me were pillars of my strength.

They shaped me into the man that was about to receive an acknowledgement from a prestigious faculty for the successful completion of their requirements for a business degree. That shape came into form from the Playmakers—Ireland--Duke Ellington— Roosevelt High School—Pennsylvania--My G.E.D.—LuLu New Orleans Café--the Firebirds—Oprah—Sunderland—Victims' Rights Advocate—Motivational Speaker--the White House—Baltimore City Health Department. As I reminisced sitting in the meetings as a director without a bachelor's degree, I lowered my head, feeling the sense of inferiority.

Was I good enough to lead them? Did my thoughts count when they have more of a formal education than I? Did they respect me? Was I good enough?

Still after the road traveled, those questions plagued my mind. Insecurity showered me. As I returned to my blessed moment, I looked around the room of draped bodies and tassels, those questions were answered. I remembered the sweet sounds of Ms. Pierre.

"Have you tried laughing?"

As I looked up, the foggy details of the crevices on Mr. Christian's smile were now clear. It was as if he was right here in the room with me. I finally made it outside to the auditorium of friends and family that have kept me flying high when everything in me, during many moments, wanted to stay low.

"William Kellibrew"

With pride, I glided up to the bridge in anticipation of shaking my University President's hand. It was not necessary for me to look out beyond the crowd and lay eyes upon Mama, the woman who had been the wind beneath my wings; or lay eyes upon the partner who had become my steady rock or lay eyes upon the friends whose support was always present. I felt their cheers from their seats. I felt the warm embrace of their smiles. I felt the pride in their whispers of yesses. I crossed over to the other side, a bachelor's degree graduate. I made no huge announcement to the world—very little was posted on social media, websites nor other mediums. It was mostly a personal accomplishment, celebrated in the quiet moments with those I hold most dear.

I continued on with my work at the health department as if nothing had occurred. I started to take notice of the credentials of those who I supervised. Many were trained social workers. I realized that though my experience in the field renders me worthy for the position I held, to truly master that which I desired to do most, I needed formal training.

Dr. Gillece also encouraged me to go back to school and get my social work degree. One time, I was asked if I had a degree in social work because of a work opportunity to review patient charts and my answer was emphatically a no. Thus, with lots of encouragement from my colleagues, I returned to hitting the books and enrolled in the Master of Social Work program.

As I was on the systems and administration pathway at the health department, I decided to pursue the clinical route in my studies. Deciding that school was going to be more intense than I anticipated, I resigned from the health department and pursued school. Such a route brings with it a required social work internship or field placement— the actual engagement with a client and systems of care.

As customary in training, preparation includes mock therapy sessions, hours of studying human behavior patterns, learning how to diagnose, and the art of interaction with one in and out of crisis. The theories and techniques vary, but as I dove deeper into my training and began my internship as a budding social worker and therapist, I encountered a client that faced insurmountable challenges. I could relate. Working hard to avoid the onset of countertransference, I studied hard at providing a safer space that invited genuine dialogue and an active ear. Much like Christine Pierre, here I was, a social work intern, navigating a multitude of theories, models, and

approaches in my head. It was all a stir! Then, I realized–mid-ses-
sion–that the William I knew so long ago, the William that sat in
the client chair, and the William that longed for someone to simply
be his friend and hear him out, was someone sitting with me and
giving me the gift of trust.

This was no training. This was a real client with real
challenges. The anxiety and lapse of time filled the space and the
air. How could I be a lifeline? How could I be the one who could
make a difference by actively listening and building rapport? I
could see in this client that they wanted one more chance–one
more chance to be treated with dignity and worth–one more
chance to be treated with respect–one more chance to choose hope.
I took a deep breath and smiled.

"Hello, my name is William Kellibrew; you can call me
Mr. Will. What would you like me to call you?"

PART III

Reflections

    As I reflected on the circle of life, I realized that my life had purpose beyond my perspective.

    It took me decades to realize that social work was a pathway that could unlock meaning and a shared perspective of social justice. It taught me about human development and behavior. It taught me about ethics and how precious the relationship is between the social worker and others, particularly clients.

    The sacred space between Ms. Christine Pierre, my first-ever therapist, taught me the power of healing and most importantly, the power of change, and that change began with me.

    I was angry with the world, angry with God, and disappointed with everyone, primarily myself. It took decades but I slowly decided to ease the burden of anxiety from my shoulders and stepped out of my fear, anger, sadness, and lack of dignity.

    I decided that my continued healing journey would require a new me and a new pathway. I was not sure where I was headed again but I renewed my faith and continued to listen to Mama tell me, "If you can handle your mother's and brother's deaths, you can handle anything. The best is yet to come."

WK

RESOURCES

EMERGENCY: If you are unsure if your situation is an emergency, call 9-1-1. The 9-1-1 dispatcher will help determine if emergency assistance is needed.

BULLYING
U.S. Department of Health and Human Services
https://www.stopbullying.gov/

DOMESTIC OR INTIMATE PARTNER VIOLENCE
https://www.thehotline.org/
1.800.799.SAFE (7233) or Text "START" to 88788

NATIONAL SEXUAL ASSAULT HOTLINE
RAINN
Call 800.656.HOPE (4673) to be connected with a trained staff member from a sexual assault service provider in your area.

SUICIDE PREVENTION
988 Suicide and Crisis Hotline
Substance Abuse and Mental Health Services Administration
https://988lifeline.org/current-events/the-lifeline-and-988/
Dial 988

VICTIM COMPENSATION
Office for Victims of Crime
U.S. Department of Justice
https://ovc.ojp.gov/topics/victim-compensation

VICTIM OF CRIME
Office for Victims of Crime
U.S. Department of Justice
https://ovc.ojp.gov/

ABOUT THE AUTHOR

William Kellibrew

Global Victim and Survivor Advocate & Author of Resilient Rose

Kellibrew has dedicated his life as a global advocate for human, civil, children and victims' rights for over 20 years. He has extensive experience in implementing trauma-informed and responsive approaches in systems of care. His work also includes a focus in victim services, violence prevention, strategic planning, and has provided expert facilitation and subject matter expertise for the Substance Abuse and Mental Health Services Administration's National Center for Trauma Informed Care and Alternatives to Seclusion and Restraints as well as the U.S. Department of Justice's Office for Victims of Crime, and the National Association of State Mental Health Program Directors' Center for Innovation in Health Policy and Practice, for more than a decade.

In 2008, Kellibrew's traumatic childhood story of resilience was featured on the Oprah Winfrey Show, CNN, MSNBC, Washington Post, Daily Beast, and a host of media outlets, globally. In 2011, Kellibrew was recognized by the White House as a 'Champion of Change' and in 2013, he received the Voice Award from SAMHSA for his work across the country as a peer leader. In 2015 he received the U.S. Congressional Survivor and Justice Caucus Eva Murillo Unsung Hero Award.

Kellibrew earned his Associate in Arts degree from the University of the District of Columbia, his Bachelor of Science degree in business management from the University of Maryland Global Campus and is in his advanced year of his Master of Social Work degree from the University of Maryland, Baltimore School of Social Work. He currently works at the Boys and Girls Clubs of America as a Safety Director for the Southeast Region, focusing on providing leadership and guidance through training, resources, consultation, and advocacy in the areas of child and club safety.

His hobbies include playing tennis, reading, creative writing, singing (including background vocals), and anything water related.

Kellibrew credits his grandmother, family, and those who created a safer space for him to heal and thrive.

MY JOURNEY

CLOCKWISE: Jacqueline Kellibrew preparing for a night on the town, Washington, D.C., circa 1970s; Jacqueline holding her son Da'Vone while playing a game of Spades, a usual friends and family gathering at her D.C. apartment, 1976; the semi-professional performing arts group gathered at Ira Aldridge Theater for their annual group photo, Washington, D.C., circa 1988, photo credit: courtesy of Kelsey E. Collie Playmakers Repertory Company; William walking the halls at age 13 while attending Langley Junior High School, Washington, D.C., 1987.

CLOCKWISE: William's only known sibling photo, (L-R) Rodney, Anthony "Tony", William "Bam Bam", Manyka "Nicci", Da'Vone, Washington, D.C., circa 1979; William at age 19, Washington, D.C., 1993; Cody, Tony, and Rodney about to head out to a casual game of football near Eastover Shopping Center, near the D.C. border with Maryland, 1982; William's siblings Da'Vone and Nicci along with their grandmother Ms. Short, gather for one of their family therapy sessions at Walter Reed Army Medical Center after a rough emotional morning start. Nicci is pregnant with her daughter Len'Nyka, 1993; William prepares for a recital in a youth residential treatment facility in Pennsylvania at age 17; William attends his 6th grade prom with a classmate at Katie C. Lewis Elementary School, Washington, D.C., 1986.

CLOCKWISE: University of Sunderland tennis team receives award at the Stadium of Light, home of the Sunderland AFC football team, (L-R) Gareth Olds, Andy Leadbetter, Gary McDonald, William Kellibrew, Sunderland, England, 2008; tennis team gathers for a team outing. (L-R) Andy Leadbetter, William Kellibrew, Gareth Olds, Paul Wales, and Michael "Pottsy" Potts, 2007; William celebrates graduating from the University of Maryland Global Campus with his bachelor's degree in business management, (L-R) Julie McMillan, Manyka Gaither, Delores Short, Brandon Wallace, Esq., Selvon Waldron, MBA, and JuRon McMillan, MBA, 2019; William leads a University of the District of Columbia historical second-ever major protest against the President of the university for an unreasonable tuition hike with fellow students Joshua Lopez, Jamal Freeman, Antonio Jones, and others, 2008.

Photo: Family archives

William Kellibrew

CLOCKWISE: University of the District of Columbia, Undergraduate Student Government Association (USGA) leaders Mah-ki Fox and Karen King de Leon join William in a Business Week magazine spread featuring student leaders, circa 2005; Sunderland City Council leader Bob Symonds welcomes newly appointed Sunderland Worldwide Ambassadors and Sister City exchange students, Elizabeth Hill (George Washington University) and William Kellibrew (University of the District of Columbia) to the City of Sunderland to the Mayor's parlor where Her Majesty Queen Elizabeth II has visited on special occasions, 2007, Photo: Courtesy of Sunderland City Council; William promotes the Next Generation of Leaders program he founded with music mogul Michael T Mauldin, Los Angeles, CA, 2013; U.D.C. USGA leaders prepare for a national student government summer preparation Historically Black College and University (HBCU) conference at Bowie State University, (L-R) Selvon Waldron, Opeyemi Oyefeso, Mah-ki Fox, Kay-Ann Willis, Rina T. Daniels, Karen King de Leon, Andrienne Huff, Daniel Mercelina, Hortense Brent, and William Kellibrew, circa 2006; Photo: Family archives; William moderates leadership discussion for the Next Generation of Leaders Teen and Youth Town Hall at the annual Tom Joyner Family Reunion in Orlando, Florida, featuring music group, Jagged Edge, singer Dondria, multiple Grammy-winning producer and artist, Brian Michael Cox, and other major artists, 2012; Photo: NXG archives.

CLOCKWISE: William joins Champions of Change working to address sexual assault and domestic violence at the White House, 2011; William keynotes the Office on Violence Against Women's Domestic Violence Awareness Month event at Great Hall at the U.S. Dept. of Justice, 2011; William opens up with his story at the first-ever hearing on childhood trauma before the U.S. Congressional Oversight and Reform Committee, 2019; William keynotes the first-ever audience domestic violence awareness event at the Navy Yard, circa 2019; William keynotes the National Candlelight Observance hosted by the Office for Victims of Crime and the U.S. Attorney General, Eric Holder , 2010; William pins AG Holder with a National Crime Victims' Rights Week badge; William's teenage hero, Charles Christian, reunite and looks on for the first time since junior high school, 2011; William prepares to keynote the OVW DV event, 2011.

CLOCKWISE: William and his grandmother, Ms. Short crisscross the United States on a speaking tour focused on family resilience following the murders of their family over 30 years ago; William walks the red carpet before receiving the Substance Abuse and Mental Health Services Administration's Peer Voice Award, 2013; William reunites with Charles C. Christian at his 94th birthday before he passed the following year; William's childhood therapist, Christine Pierre hears William speak at the Distinguished Speaker Series at the University of the District of Columbia's School of Business; Christine Pierre attends and speaks at the William Kellibrew Foundation's Annual Holiday and Benefit Concert, now in its 11th year at Berean Baptist Church in Washington, D.C.

CLOCKWISE: William emcees a Phi Beta Sigma Fraternity, Inc. event on Capitol Hill honoring the late and Honorable U.S. Congress member, John R. Lewis; William receives a mayoral resolution in Baltimore City at the Healing Neen Trauma-Informed Conference, circa 2020; William shares his story with audiences across the United States.

"MAMA"

CLOCKWISE: Ms. Short (Mama) and Ms. Susie Stevens, concert coordinator, for the Annual Holiday and Benefit Concert for the William Kellibrew Foundation, enjoy an annual intimate dinner at Farmers and Distillers in Washington, D.C. after the concert, 2018; Ms. Short smiles and sits for an interview for an upcoming documentary about her family's resilience following the murders of her daughter and grandson over 30 years ago, 2022; Ms. Short and JuRon McMillan, board director, WKF, support William as he testifies before Congress on the impact of childhood trauma, 2019; William and his grandmother make a pitstop in New York City, one of her favorite places to visit while on a speaking tour, 2017; William prepares for his Congressional testimony in Washington, D.C.

WK